Martial Arts
Are Not
Just for Kicking Butt

Martial Arts Are Not Just for Kicking Butt

An Anthology of Writings on Martial Arts

Edited by

Antonio Cuevas and Jennifer Lee

North Atlantic Books
Berkeley, California

Martial Arts Are Not Just for Kicking Butt:
An Anthology of Writings on Martial Arts

Published by
North Atlantic Books
P.O. Box 12327
Berkeley, California 94712
www.northatlanticbooks.com

Cover art by Sharilyn Neidhardt
Cover and book design by Catherine E. Campaigne

Printed in the United States of America

This is issue number 59 in the *Io* series

Martial Arts Are Not Just for Kicking Butt: An Anthology of Writings on Martial Arts is sponsored by the Society for the Study of Native Arts and Sciences, a nonprofit educational corporation whose goals are to develop an educational and crosscultural perspective linking various scientific, social, and artistic fields; to nurture a holistic view of arts, sciences, humanities, and healing; and to publish and distribute literature on the relationship of mind, body, and nature.

Library of Congress Cataloging-in-Publication Data

Martial arts are not just for kicking butt : an anthology of writings on
    martial arts / edited by Antonio Cuevas, Jennifer Lee
        p.   cm.
    ISBN 1-55643-266-6
    1. Martial arts.   2. Martial arts-Philosophy.   I. Cuevas, Antonio.
    II. Lee, Jennifer, 1971–   .
    CG1101.M28   1998
    796.8-dc21   97-50055
                                                          CIP

1   2   3   4   5   6   7   8   9   /   01   00   99   98

∫

Permissions

Bira Almeida, "Jôgo de Capoeira" from *Capoeira: A Brazilian Art Form,* 1986. North Atlantic Books, ISBN 0-938190-29-6, $14.95. Reprinted by permission of the author.

Rene Denfeld, "Are Women the Weaker Sex?" from *Kill the Body, The Head Will Fall.* Copyright © 1997 by Rene Denfeld. All rights reserved. Reprinted by permission of Warner Books, Inc., New York, NY, USA.

Ben Downing, "Jôgo Bonito." Previously appeared in *Southwest Review:* Autumn 1996. Reprinted by permission of the author.

John F. Gilbey, "Master of Applied Cowardice" from *The Way of a Warrior: A Journey into Secret Worlds of Martial Arts,* 1982. North Atlantic Books, ISBN 1-55643-126-0, $12.95. Reprinted by permssion of the author.

Richard Grossinger, "T'ai Chi Tales" excerpts from *Out of Babylon: Ghosts of Grossinger's,* 1997. Frog, Ltd., ISBN 1-883319-57-9, $18.95. Reprinted by permission of the author.

Richard Strozzi Heckler, "The Invitation" from *In Search of the Warrior Spirit: Teaching Awareness Disciplines to the Green Berets,* 1990. North Atlantic Books, ISBN 1-55643-116-3, $16.95. Reprinted by permission of the author.

George Plimpton, chapter 9 from *Shadow Box,* 1993. Lions & Burford Publishing, ISBN 1-558212-76-0, $14.95. Reprinted by permission of the author.

Masayuki Shimabukuro and Leonard J. Pellman, "Jinseikan" from *Flashing Steel: Mastering Eishin-Ryu Swordsmanship,* 1995. Frog, Ltd., ISBN 1-883319-18-8, $18.95. Reprinted by permission of the authors.

Ron Sieh, excerpt from *Martial Arts For Beginners,* 1995. Writers and Readers Publishing, Inc., ISBN 0-86316-171-5, $11.00. Reprinted by permission of Writers and Readers Publishing, Inc., P.O. Box 461 Village Station, New York, NY 10014, USA.

Bruce Thomas, "The Roots of Combat" from *Bruce Lee: Fighting Spirit,* 1994. Frog, Ltd., ISBN 1-883319-25-0, $12.95. Reprinted by permission of the author.

Carol A. Wiley, "From Fatso to Breakfalls" from *Women in the Martial Arts,* 1992. North Atlantic Books, ISBN 1-55643-136-8, $12.95. Reprinted by permission of the author.

Contents

vii

CONTENTS

ix

Introduction

To many, the martial arts are defined as the fighting arts. From fighting artists, we expect fancy and efficient blows, cuts and kicks that slam opponents across the room and against the wall before the opponent is even fully aware of what's happening. However, in the following collection of writings, fighting may be a misleading word because we are not referring to the fighting of barroom brawls and mean street rumbles. What we refer to are those martial practices that have made an art of the struggle, where the struggle becomes an artful discipline and where the fighter becomes an artist.

Whether experienced or new to the martial arts, readers can expect an inviting spectrum of narratives on martial training in this collection—from the historical, philosophical, and sociopolitical to the intensely personal. All of the pieces are, in the end, candid accounts that should raise second thoughts about the clichés of kicking butt with martial techniques.

The writers we have chosen to showcase in this anthology

have succeeded in tackling the unexpected challenges in what it is to discipline and strengthen one's fight. What may surprise readers is that the struggle or fight against an opponent is really the easiest of struggles a martial artist needs to overcome. Understanding your mind's will and your body's strength, your range of limitations and possibilities are the foremost challenges of practicing martial arts.

In the report by George Plimpton, Muhammad Ali travels through the segregated South on his infamous red tour bus. Though seemingly less interested in the controversial issues surrounding integration than his trainer and friend, Bundini, Ali explicitly chooses to bus through the South, rather than fly over it. As "champion of the whole wide world," Ali nonetheless hesitates entering any world that makes it a point to humiliate and subjugate him because of the color of his skin. Yet in his own ambivalent way, with a little push from Bundini to take respite in a Georgia diner, he makes his statement and his stand. Ali triumphs not by knocking out racists, but by using the discipline of a great martial artist to temper his actions.

In "Are Women the Weaker Sex?" Rene Denfeld, amateur female boxer, demonstrates the strength of a woman's body. Not surprisingly, she confronts chauvinistic ideas about women in the ring, but unexpectedly, not so much from fellow male boxers as from the men who watch from outside the ring: the fans, her brother. . . .

In the same way that Denfeld discusses the female element of 'the sweet science' of boxing, Richard Heckler introduces the polemics of teaching a movement/energy art like aikido to a group of elite American warrior-troopers. Invited by the U.S. Army to train the Green Berets in aikido and meditation, Heckler not only struggles with his own hesitations but the adamant opposition of liberal friends who witnessed the military operations of the Vietnam era.

While reading these writings on the martial arts, we are most intrigued by the articulation of the struggle within, as much as the battle that takes place with another. The martial arts are practical tools for these writers, but they have also become metaphors for life. Themes of struggle-within/struggle-without are present in many places, not just the martial arts, because they express what is constant in our lives. In the words of Terry Dobson, from "Terry Dobson Yawns in Slumber," *Fighting my brother is fighting myself. . . . So make a brother of your enemy.* Easier said than done when your toughest enemy is yourself, but likewise, your greatest victory may await within yourself—on the battlefield, on the mat, in an open field, in your own life.

The Editors
Berkeley, California
April 1998

Part I

JINSEIKAN: Iaijutsu Philosophy

Masayuki Shimabukuro and Leonard J. Pellman

It is highly unlikely that you will ever slip into your *hakama*, sling your *katana* at your side, and saunter down the street prepared to use your *iaijutsu* skills to defend yourself or take up the cause of the downtrodden like the samurai of old. So what benefit is there in iaijutsu training?

The fact that you will probably never engage in a real sword battle may, paradoxically, be the *greatest* benefit of sword training! Those who train in martial arts that have modern practical application, such as karate-do or jiujutsu, too often find themselves so involved in developing skill in the physical self-defense applications of their art that they overlook or minimize their mental and spiritual training. Especially in the West, martial arts training often merely gives lip-service to these vital elements of training. This cannot be said of iaijutsu.

By its very nature, as a martial art that is highly ritualized, moderately paced, and without obvious "street" application, iaijutsu provides an ideal environment in which to refine mental and spiritual discipline. *All* martial arts are supposed to develop these qualities, but few adequately emphasize them in modern practice.

This is not to say that iaijutsu is neither practical nor beneficial—far from it! Iaijutsu develops qualities which are not only useful for self-defense, if needed, but also improve one's experience of daily life. For this reason, training in this seemingly "impractical" art is far more practical than learning "street-fighting" techniques for anyone but a thug.

BUDO NO ARIKATA:
Purpose of Martial Arts

To understand the purpose of martial arts training, we need only understand the goal of martial arts: to *win!*

It is that simple.

At the same time, it is far more complex. Obviously, we learn a martial art in order to prevail in an encounter. We certainly don't spend years training in order to be defeated! However, martial arts training involves much more than merely learning how to injure or kill another person in battle.

A Japanese legend relates that, centuries ago, there were two samurai who were closer than brothers. As they matured and prepared to embark on their *musha shugyo*—the customary travels to perfect their skills—it was apparent that their paths would separate for many years. So before departing, they met by a quiet stream and vowed to meet again on that very spot twelve years later to share tales of their training and exploits. Just as they had vowed, they returned to the bank of the stream on the very day twelve years later, but found that a recent rain had swollen the gentle stream into a raging torrent, barring their way to the exact spot of their last meeting.

Determined to live up to the letter and spirit of his vow, and to demonstrate the incredible skills he had mastered during their twelve-year separation, one samurai dashed to the river and made a spectacular leap that carried him over the deadly current and safely to the other side. The jump far exceeded today's Olympic records, and should have amazed his friend. Instead, the other samurai calmly walked a few paces upstream and hired a boatman to row him across for 5 *mon* (about 50 cents).

The skills one man spent a lifetime of sacrifice and dedication to develop could be duplicated effortlessly for a few pennies. Similarly, if our goal is merely to kill people, we can simply purchase a gun, rather than invest years of training. So, the first lesson of iaijutsu is to be certain that your training goals are worthwhile.

Next, we must realize that "winning" is not merely defeating an opponent; it is perfecting yourself—your personal character, as well as your skills—to the degree that an opponent cannot prevail against you. Yet, winning is still more than this.

In iaijutsu, there is a saying: *"Kachi wa saya no naka ni ari"* ("Victory comes while the sword is [still] in the scabbard"). Physical skills alone, no matter how highly perfected, are simply not enough. There is always someone more skillful, or someone with a dirty trick for which you are unprepared. But *attitude* is more important than *aptitude* in real combat. We have all seen encounters reminiscent of that between David and Goliath, where the underdog defeats a far mightier opponent through sheer determination and faith.

Without the courage or determination to use it, a high degree of skill is useless. It would be like painting a great masterpiece, then storing it away where no one can ever see it. This is not only a waste of time, talent, and effort, but a loss of something valuable to humankind.

So the higher purpose of iaijutsu is to develop the mind and spirit of a warrior, an attitude and strength of character that wins the battle before it begins. This is no simple matter to achieve. It takes years of daily training to cultivate these attributes and to rid oneself of attitudes and reactions, such as anger, fear, selfishness, jealousy, and hate, that are counterproductive or self-destructive.

Furthermore, winning must be accomplished without *trying to win!* Once again, this concept at first seems self-contradictory. After all, how can you be victorious if you don't even try to win? The answer is that the key to winning a battle is a steadfast determination to *not lose.*

This is more than just a semantic difference; it requires a profound shift of focus and commitment. When you are trying to win, you will be inclined to take unnecessary risks in your determination to defeat your opponent. But when you are instead dedicated to not losing the encounter, you have the luxury of waiting for your opponent to make a mistake that you can then exploit to achieve victory.

However, iaijutsu training demands a still higher and more noble purpose than merely winning (or not losing) battles. The great Chinese tactician Lao Tsu said that the highest principle in the Art of War is to *win without a battle.* This is the true ideal of iaijutsu, as embodied in the Chinese ideograms for "martial art":

BU
"Martial"

JUTSU
"Art"

The symbol on the left, above, which we translate as "martial" (the *"bu"* in *budo*) was formed from the two characters below:

TOMERU
"Prevent"

HOKO
"Conflict"

Thus, the term "martial arts," from the earliest of times, has truly meant "The Art of Conflict Prevention." The way iaijutsu training accomplishes this goal can only be discovered by understanding the underlying ideals of the martial arts.

SHUGYO NO MOKUTEKI: *Ideals of Martial Arts*

Japan's most famous and revered samurai, Miyamoto Musashi, once asked his young disciple, Jotaro, what his goal in life was. Without hesitation, the teenager replied, "To be like *you!*"

"Your goal is too small," Musashi scolded him. He went on to admonish his student to "aspire to be like Mt. Fuji, with such a broad and solid foundation that the strongest earthquake cannot move you, and so tall that the greatest enterprises of common men seem insignificant from your lofty perspective. With your mind as high as Mt. Fuji," he explained, "you can see all things clearly. And you can see all the forces which shape events; not just the things happening near you."

Walking together along a twisting mountain path, Musashi and Jotaro soon came to a bend at which an enormous overhanging boulder loomed above the path. At first glance, the boulder seemed precariously suspended above them, as if the slightest jar would break it loose and send it crashing down to annihilate them. Yet, a closer look showed it to be so firmly embedded in the mountainside that it would take the forces of nature eons to work it free. Nevertheless, Jotaro scuttled nervously along the path beneath it, anxious to be out from under it. As Musashi calmly followed, he noticed his disciple's natural reaction to the threatening presence of the massive rock, and used it to reinforce his lesson.

"You should train to become like this boulder," Musashi told Jotaro, "With most of your strength hidden, and so deeply rooted that you are immovable. Yet, so powerful that what can be seen will make men cringe to walk in your shadow."

This, Musashi felt, was the ultimate goal of training: to be so highly skilled and mentally developed that your mere presence was intimidating and no man would dare challenge you. And, indeed, Musashi reached, even exceeded, this level of personal development during his colorful life. Clearly, someone this highly trained will have to fight few, if any, battles to achieve life's victories.

Later in life, it was this very quality that Musashi looked for in selecting a student to train. After he had retired to refine his character through the arts of painting, sculpting, and calligraphy, Musashi accepted an invitation by the Kumamoto *daimyo* to come to his castle and train an elite corps of samurai to become the *daimyo*'s personal retainers. So great was the *daimyo*'s respect for Musashi that he had all of his samurai—several hundred of them— form a processional line on both sides of the street, extending from the castle gates to the town. As Musashi strode between the two columns of men, each bowed reverently at his passage. But, as Musashi's keen eye detected, even these elite samurai averted their gaze from his bold stare. Only one among them seemed not to be intimated by Musashi's mere countenance.

When Musashi finally reached the *daimyo* and his counselors, the *daimyo* asked if any of his samurai had particularly impressed Musashi, perhaps testing to see if Musashi could discern his most skillful swordsmen at just a passing glance. Musashi led the *daimyo* back to the one man who had not cast his eyes down as Musashi passed.

"This man!" Musashi announced.

"I don't understand," the *daimyo* blustered, "He has little training and only modest rank. In fact, his main duty is stone cutting for the castle."

"This may be so," Musashi answered, "But he is your best trained samurai." Turning to the man, Musashi asked him, "Tell me, how do you train that you have no fear of death?"

"I hardly train at all," the samurai admitted humbly, "When I go to bed each night, I simply unsheathe my sword and hang it above my face by a slender thread. Then I lie down beneath it and gaze up at its point until I fall asleep."

"This is indeed your best trained samurai," Musashi told the *daimyo,* with a knowing smile. "He alone of all your men faces death every day, for he knows that it would take little for that tiny thread to break and end his life. I will train *this* man to be your personal bodyguard."

However, as Musashi continued to mature, he found—to his great dismay—that even such an incredible level of personal development was not enough. Despite the fact that even the bravest samurai could not bear to gaze upon Musashi in awe of him, he was still challenged many times and forced to kill more than sixty opponents in sword duels. He found that his reputation and his aura of power and invincibility attracted fame-seekers like moths to a flame. Obviously, anyone who could defeat the legendary Miyamoto Musashi would be instantly famous, able to found his own school of swordsmanship, and command riches, position, and prestige as a high-ranking retainer to any *daimyo*, or perhaps even the shogun. So, throughout most of his life, Musashi found himself beleaguered by challengers betting their lives against a chance at such fame and fortune.

Several years after his encounter with the Kumamoto *daimyo*, Musashi was once again in the mountains seeking to perfect his character. Together with his life-long friend and mentor, the priest Soho Takuan, he was seated beside a gentle stream with a small, tranquil waterfall, engaged in *zazen* meditation. As they meditated, Musashi's keen senses alerted him to another presence nearby. Without disturbing the serenity of his meditation, Musashi allowed his gaze to fall upon a deadly viper slithering into the clearing from some shrubbery near Takuan.

Knowing that the slightest movement might frighten the venomous snake into attacking his friend, Musashi carefully controlled his spirit, watching the serpent in utter stillness. He was surprised to see a faint smile appear on Takuan's lips as he, too, became aware of the snake's approach and calmly watched it crawl across his own thighs. Even more amazing than the priest's complete tranquillity in the face of mortal danger was the snake's casual acceptance of Takuan as a natural part of its surroundings.

After slithering across the priest, the lethal serpent continued on its winding course toward Musashi. But, several feet away, the snake sensed Musashi's presence and recoiled, preparing to attack the seated samurai. Musashi gave no reaction. Even though his spirit was undisturbed by the ominous, bared fangs of the viper, Musashi's power, skill, and menace were so palpable to the snake that it scurried away into the bushes like a terrified rabbit. Most men would have been proud to possess such an intimidating aura, but Musashi felt only shame as he suddenly understood his own greatest shortcoming.

"What troubles you so?" asked Takuan, sensing his friend's mood.

"All my life," Musashi lamented, "I have trained myself to develop such skill that no man would ever dare attack me. And now that I have reached my goal, all living things instinctively fear me. You saw how the snake fled from me!"

"I saw it," the priest said. "Since it dared not attack you, you defeated it without striking a blow. And because of your great skill, both you *and* the snake are alive now." Although he already knew the answer, Takuan asked, "Why does that sadden you?"

"Because I am so strong that no one can ever grow close to me. I can never have true peace." Musashi pointed a finger at the priest. "Not like you," he said with admiration. "You did not fear the snake, nor did the snake fear you. Your spirit is so calm, so natural, that the snake treated you no differently than the rocks, the trees, or the wind. *People* accept you that way, too."

Takuan only smiled, pleased that his friend had made such an important self-discovery.

Musashi spent the rest of his days training to perfect a spirit like that of his friend Takuan. This mental state, the ideal to which all martial artists aspire, is called *heijoshin*. Literally translated, it means "constant stable spirit," but such a translation hardly does it justice. The nuances of the Japanese language help greatly in understanding the full nature of heijoshin, a word comprised of three *kanji* (ideograms):

| Hei | Jo | Shin |

Hei has numerous related meanings in Japanese: "peaceful," "calm," "steady," and so on. The closest English equivalent, however, may be "level" or "even," since these terms can be used in such ways as "level-headed" and "even-handed" in English.

Jo has a more precise meaning, at least in terms of its English translations: "always," "constant," or "continually."

11

₪ *Shin* translates both literally and figuratively as "heart," with almost all the same nuances. Thus, to Asians and Westerners alike, *shin* is understood as more than simply the internal organ that pumps blood, but connotes the mind, the spirit, the emotions, the character—the whole inner essence of the individual.

Thus, heijoshin is a concept of the whole inner being of a person being continually at peace. For lack of a more effective translation, we will simply call it "peace of mind." However, the fullness of heijoshin warrants a more detailed explanation.

HEIJOSHIN:
Peace of Mind

Heijoshin, *true* peace of mind, is probably best understood, not as a single attribute but as a combination—or rather the *culmination*—of several character traits. Each of the aspects that together create heijoshin may take years of effort, experience, and disappointment to develop, making heijoshin the product of a lifetime of patient training. To achieve genuine peace of mind requires a high degree of mental development in three key areas: (1) the intellect, (2) the emotions, and (3) that indefinable element we usually call "character" or "integrity." And these three areas must be developed *in balance.*

Why is heijoshin so important?

As we age, our physical prowess, no matter how great, will eventually lessen. This is especially evident in professional sports, where few athletes enjoy a career longer than ten years. But, with diligence, our character and our mental prowess will constantly improve. And we can never be certain that ill health or a serious accident might not leave us with drastically impaired physical ability, while our mental faculties remain strong. The key to lifelong fruitfulness and happiness, then, is not in our physical skills, but in our mental development.

This is why cultivating heijoshin is far more important to the martial artist than merely perfecting skill with a sword. Furthermore, heijoshin is an unlimited quality. There is always room for more knowledge, greater compassion, stronger love, and a higher level of character development.

How do you obtain heijoshin?

Heijoshin is not only difficult to attain, but there is no simple, precise method to develop it. This is a stumbling block to many Westerners, especially in America, where people have become culturally conditioned to a "quick-fix" approach to nearly everything. If something cannot be achieved with a wonder drug, an overnight miracle, or a three-step/five-day program, it seems too difficult and time-consuming to attempt.

So, to begin with, you might as well understand that heijoshin demands a lifestyle change: a life of discipline, effort, sacrifice, and commitment. Such a commitment to developing excellence of character sets the martial artist—particularly the iaijutsu practitioner—apart from most people in a confused and unhappy society.

Not only is there no easy way to develop heijoshin, but for each of us the path will be different, because of our different personalities, experiences, and circumstances. To further complicate matters, heijoshin is rife with paradoxes. The first of these is the nature of heijoshin itself: it is the product of diligent training and continual effort to reshape the mind, yet in the end it must be completely natural and unforced.

So, how do we practice something which must occur spontaneously?

The tales of Miyamoto Musashi told earlier in this chapter contain some clues that may help answer this question. If you read them again now, you may notice that Musashi did not train himself in the "art" of heijoshin itself, but rather in the elements

13

which lead to its development. In effect, in another of its para-doxes, while heijoshin is the true goal of martial arts training, it is achieved as a *by-product* of training.

If heijoshin was merely a single attribute, it could be practiced and learned, like multiplication tables. But, since it is itself the by-product of a person's complete inner being, it can only be achieved by refining that whole inner essence. And this can only be accomplished if one's intellect, emotions, and character are developed *in balance.*

Why is martial arts training the best method for developing heijoshin?

When a person realizes the true nature of martial arts training, and practices accordingly, it leads to a fuller understanding of the nature of life itself. Martial arts are essentially concerned with life and death. This is most apparent, perhaps, in iaijutsu training, since the outcome of a sword battle is clearly that one opponent lives and the other dies. This is not the case with karate-do or other "empty-hand" arts, in which the "loser" might merely be rendered incapable of continuing the fight.

So if the iaijutsu student is serious about his or her training, each *kata* (practice pattern) represents far more than simply swing-ing a sword around. It is a symbolic battle in which your oppo-nent will most certainly die. Will you end his life without good cause? Will you throw his family into turmoil, and perhaps ruin, over some triviality? When you have developed true compassion for others, then train in a life-or-death context, you gain a whole new appreciation for life—both your own and the lives of others.

Isn't "life-or-death" training unrealistic in modern society?

The sad fact is that few people, other than the best-trained mar-tial artists, truly understand how tenuous life is. The samurai understood this, because he was trained to realize that each new day might bring death. The pioneers of the Old West understood it, because of the tremendous hardships and uncertainties they faced. But, in an age in which hunger, disease, and most of our mortal enemies have been all but vanquished, we seem to have become blinded to the precariousness of our existence. Even when we read of a major celebrity succumbing to AIDS, or a terrible plane crash, or a terrorist bombing, or a drive-by gang shooting, most of us believe that "it can't happen to me."

The life-or-death awareness of iaijutsu training allows us to clearly see that death is, quite literally, only one heartbeat away. Part of heijoshin is coming to grips with the inevitability of death. That it will eventually claim the "high" and "low" alike—movie stars, drug addicts, sports heroes, bank robbers, politicians, business executives, and even ourselves.

Once we understand how fragile our life is, we have a vital choice to make. We can either live in seclusion, like Howard Hughes in his later years, cowering in paranoid fear of everything from germs to fatal accidents, or we can determine to live each moment we are given to the fullest and die with no regrets.

Yet it is only after deciding to live life to its fullest, that we have the most difficult choices to make. It is then that we must come to grips with what brings true and lasting happiness and fulfillment to life.

If you were given only one week to live, what would you do? Would you live out your final days in a wild, uninhibited bacchanalia of sensual pleasures? Many would. Would you sell all that you had accumulated and spend your last week donating to every worthy cause you could think of? That would be more noble. Would you feverishly attend to every detail of settling your estate, so your loved ones would be provided for after your death? That would demonstrate a high degree of responsibility and integrity. Would you spend every moment possible with your family and closest friends? That would probably give your final hours the greatest comfort. Or would you do nothing different than you had done the previous week, or the week before that? *That* would indicate that your lifestyle has produced heijoshin!

This brings us to another paradox: If you have achieved heijoshin, you will live every day as if it was your last. But just because you live every day as if it was your last does not mean you have attained heijoshin. It is not simply "living like there's no tomorrow" that demonstrates heijoshin, but *how* you live your last day that is the barometer of your character. It is the quality and purpose of your life that gives it value.

How should I live my life to have heijoshin?

The highest principle of heijoshin is to develop your mind (the combination of intellect, emotions, and character) to such an elevated state that you are unaffected by your environment. This is what Musashi was trying to impress upon Jotaro by admonishing him to train himself to be like Mt. Fuji. It means not allowing circumstances to control your emotions, nor emotions to confuse your judgment.

If your happiness and security are based primarily upon your financial status, then you will only be comfortable when things are going well. If you lose your job and begin to have difficulty paying your bills, soon you will find yourself constantly under stress, doubting your own abilities and value, and angered by the loss of the material freedom you once had. In the end, you will likely find yourself taking a job that is not right for you, just to regain your self-esteem and recover your lost financial status. This is an example of your circumstances controlling your emotions, and your emotions in turn confusing your judgment.

But, if your contentment is derived from knowing the type of person that you are *inside,* then you will more readily understand that life has its ups and downs. You will realize that the sun rises upon the evil and the good, and the rain falls upon the righteous and the unrighteous alike. Everyone experiences an occasional windfall, and no one is exempt from times of hardship, so it is foolish to allow these circumstances to dictate your emotions. What is more, the rich and famous are often the unhappiest people in the world, while the so-called "lowly," like Mother Teresa, enjoy a rich and fulfilling life. Once you understand that it is what you *are,* not what you *have,* that is important, you are able to rise above your circumstances.

The second key tenet of heijoshin is to understand that you are part of your environment, that what you are and what you do has an effect on other people. Even your emotions affect others. If you are discouraged, you will drop a cloud of gloom on the people with whom you come in contact. If you are joyful, just the sight of you will gladden them. If you behave rudely, you will anger people or hurt their feelings. If you are pleasant and respectful, you will brighten their day. People who look up to you will follow your example, whether it is good or bad.

This presents another of heijoshin's paradoxes:

How can we be unaffected by our environment when we are *part* of our environment?

Obviously, our environment *will* affect us to some degree. The state of the economy will affect us, our health will affect us, the actions of friends and loved ones will affect us. Heijoshin is not a condition in which we insulate ourselves from our surroundings, nor deny that our problems exist, nor deaden our minds and senses to our feelings. Heijoshin is not a means of escape, like drugs, which allows you to ignore or be unaware of your emotions. Quite the opposite, to possess heijoshin demands that you be deeply in touch with your emotions. It is perfectly natural to *feel* anger, joy, disappointment, love, and the full range of emotions. Heijoshin, however, allows us not to be *controlled* by these emotions, so that our actions are not determined by a fleeting impulse, but are the products of a consistent, balanced, and focused mind.

How can I experience my emotions, yet not let them affect my actions?

The answer comes from developing two essential character traits: *understanding* and *compassion*.

First, you must understand yourself; understand *why* you feel the way you do, why certain events or situations evoke certain emotions in you. Then, you must have compassion for yourself. Accept yourself for what you are, and why you are what you are. You cannot change who you are now. You have already become that person. You can only change who you will be in the future. If you condemn yourself for your faults and failures, it is only a waste of your emotional energy and destructive to your self-esteem. But, if you can compassionately accept yourself as you are now, then you have a positive starting point from which to begin developing into the person you want to become.

Second, you must have the same understanding and compassion for others. Once you have thoroughly understood yourself, you can appreciate that other people have become who they are for a reason. There have been influences and circumstances that have shaped them into the people they have become. By compassionately accepting others with both their strengths and weaknesses, you will be able to distinguish between your feelings toward the *person* and your feelings about their *behavior*. This separation is vital to human relationships.

If someone behaves rudely, for example, I can either become offended at the *person* or at the person's *behavior*. If I become offended at the person, my natural reaction will be to avoid that offensive person. If, instead, I look beyond the person and see the behavior as offensive, then my natural reaction will be to try to understand what caused it, because I am now viewing the situation as an offensive action committed by an acceptable person. Rather than shunning the person, I will try to communicate with him or her, and my reaction will be motivated by concern rather than anger or resentment.

Westerners reflect an understanding of this aspect of heijoshin in this commonly quoted prayer:

"God grant me the serenity to accept the things I cannot change, the courage to change the things I can, and the wisdom to know the difference."

When should I use heijoshin?

Heijoshin is not something you turn on and off like a politician's smile. Once heijoshin is rooted in you, it is with you at all times everywhere you go, from the time you wake up to the time you go to bed—even while you are sleeping! It becomes your natural state of mind, not something you summon only when you "need" it.

What are the benefits of heijoshin?

Obviously, by developing a constant, peaceful state of mind, you, as an individual, will lead a happier, more serene life, freed from bondage to an emotional roller coaster propelled by forces beyond your control. But the benefits of heijoshin cannot remain exclusively personal. By its nature, heijoshin cannot exist in a vacuum, so its benefits will spread from you to society as a whole.

Society is simply a collection of individuals. Social ills, like crime and drug abuse, are merely the reflection of the combined failings of the individuals who comprise society. Laws cannot reform society and cure its ills, they can only punish violators. Society is like our collective shadow. If the shadow is bent and twisted, no amount of effort can straighten it. Only by straightening ourselves does our shadow also straighten, and then it does so effortlessly and automatically. So it is that reform must start with individuals and spread through society. It is a "grass roots" process in which each of us is either part of the disease or part of the cure.

If our behavior is controlled by our circumstances and emotions, rather than by our strength of character and ideals, then we are part of the disease. If, instead, our heijoshin lifts us above our circumstances and helps us live with greater purpose and meaning, our example will inspire others to become part of the cure.

Thus, the ultimate objective of heijoshin is the same as the ultimate objective of martial arts: **to help each individual reach his or her full potential, and thereby improve society as a whole.**

SHUGYO NO HAJIME:
The Journey's Beginning

Having determined to set out on this journey of self-discovery and perfection of character through martial arts training, you need to know where to start. As good as any book or video may be, you cannot learn martial arts from it alone. Martial arts instruction is personal. It is nothing like learning spelling or arithmetic in school.

True martial arts instruction—the development, maturing, and shaping of a good *budoka* (martial artist)—is not a process; it is a *relationship*. For that reason, it requires a good instructor and a good *dojo* (school). The depth of understanding of both the physical and philosophical aspects of iaijutsu can only be passed on through a mentor relationship. This is why the Japanese place such importance—bordering on reverence—on the close relationship between a *seito* (student) and his *sensei* (teacher), and in the relationship between *sempai* (senior students) and *kohai* (junior students).

A *sensei* is more than merely a martial arts instructor, he is the model of technical and philosophical excellence to which his students aspire. The *sempai,* or senior student, is a partner in the training process who acts like a nurturing older brother or sister, guiding and encouraging the student on the often difficult and disappointing road toward his or her objectives and ideals.

Dojo literally means "Place of the Way." It is not just a building in which to practice martial arts; it is a laboratory in which to study, experiment, and refine a complete and fulfilling *way of life.* You should select your dojo with the utmost care, as though your life, or at least the *quality* of your life, depended on it.

The first step, therefore, in reaching your full potential is to find a good sensei teaching in a good dojo. Remember that a good player is not always a good coach, so you must look not only at the instructor's technical expertise, but at his ability to lead, instruct, and inspire his students. Some good measures of these abilities are the degree of respect shown by his students, whether the senior students show a nurturing attitude toward their juniors, and whether the students are able to acquire the skills and—more importantly—the *attitudes* the instructor is trying to impart.

The only way to do this is to visit those dojo in your area which have the highest reputation among respected budoka. Visit each one in which you are interested several times to observe classes and discuss your training goals with the instructor. You should not only determine if the instructor's teaching style is suited to your personality and the way you best learn, but pay particular attention to his attitude and demeanor. Does he exhibit the highest ideals of martial arts in the way he conducts himself? Does he become disinterested in you if you don't join his dojo right away? Does he show more concern for you as a potential student, or in your ability to pay for the lessons? The "bottom-line" question to ask yourself is: "Is this sensei the kind of role model I want to emulate?"

Once you have selected a dojo, it is important for you to seek a close relationship with your sensei. After all, iaijutsu training is training for everyday life, so in order for it to take root, *your training must be part of your everyday life and your daily life must be part of your training.* The Japanese have a saying, *"Shi-Tei Nu Ni"* ("Master and Disciple are not Two"), meaning that your *sensei* should be like a wise, patient parent to you. Seek the counsel of your sensei concerning the opportunities, issues, and problems you are facing, so that he or she can show you how to apply sound martial arts principles to them.

Lastly, *train seriously.* Use your imagination to "feel" your opponent and face death through your training. As you learn to vividly face death while you practice iaijutsu, your eyes will be opened to what life is really about!

IKA NI SHINUKA:
How to Die Well

An extremely significant part of a samurai's training was learning to die well. As we have emphasized repeatedly, facing death—either vicariously in the dojo, or literally on the battlefield—was a daily routine for the samurai. Part of a samurai's training included instruction in the proprieties of ritualistic suicide (*seppuku*), accomplished by slitting open his own abdomen. A samurai was also trained and prepared to act as *kaishaku,* or assistant, in the event one of his peers was called upon to commit *seppuku,* and was well-versed in both the technique and etiquette of this crucial role. Even a woman of samurai rank was prepared to perform ritual suicide, albeit by a more genteel method, by slitting her throat.

One of the hallmarks of a samurai was his avowed purpose: *"Shinu kikai o motomo"* ("Looking for the opportunity to die"). In the West, we often seem to interpret this as an exaggerated sense of fatalism among the samurai—a view which reduces them to little more than half-crazed warriors throwing themselves wantonly into battle as if their lives were worthless.

While applying the principle of *shinu kikai o motomo* did free the samurai to face his enemy with fearless disregard for his own life, it was not for the reason suggested by this shallow interpretation. Instead, the samurai held his life to be of great value. It was therefore to be lost—or even risked—only if the cause was worthy of such a noble and extreme sacrifice!

Thus, in searching for the opportunity to die, the samurai really sought the reason to live. As modern samurai we should do no less. Facing death in our training helps us to focus on those things that are *truly* important to our lives, such as family, personal relationships, strength of character, and so forth. In this way, *shinu kikai o motomo* leads us to decide what is really worth living for.

When we begin to focus our thoughts, ideals, and desires in this manner, most of the complexities, gray areas, and dilemmas of life are removed from our path. We no longer allow the trivialities and distractions which so complicate most people's lives to be a factor in ours.

By becoming a complete martial artist—a person who understands *Budo no Arikata* and *Shugyo no Mokuteki,* who possesses heijoshin and has determined their *shinu kikai o motomo*—we will know what truly victorious living is. We will live a life *worth living,* a life with purpose and meaning, filled with rich, intimate relationships. And when we reach the end of our appointed days, we will be able to look back on our lives without regrets.

This is the true purpose of iaijutsu training.

"I had heard somewhere that Muhammad Ali ..."

George Plimpton

I had heard somewhere that Muhammad Ali (by this time he had changed his name) would be driving his bus and his whole entourage of sparring partners and cooks and hangers-on from Miami to Chicopee Falls, Massachusetts, where he planned to set up his prefight training for the second Sonny Liston fight, and that there were seats available if any sports journalists wanted to come along for the ride. I arranged a spot for myself, flew down from New York and took a taxi out to where the bus was waiting at Ali's place in North Miami.

Just before we set off, the new champion stood on the bus steps and made a short speech in which he described the blessings those on the trip (there were four journalists, counting myself) would enjoy: food, coffee, the new heavyweight champion at the wheel; he would tell us jokes, do dance routines and other entertainments; and he had only one request—that we all eat heavily before crossing the state line into Georgia, because we weren't going to be "flying" over the state. I didn't know what he meant at the time.

We set off. Ali called his bus Big Red, which was one of Malcolm X's nicknames, but the bus was more likely named for its gaudy circus-wagon color. Inside, Ali had picked the decor—an eye-tiring silver roof with uneven patterns of burnished gold. Some of the seats had their supports removed so that they collapsed back on the seat behind; in them the sparring partners slept a lot, lying on their backs with their big hands folded comfortably on their coverall fronts. One of them was Cody Jones, whom everyone called the Porcupine for his swept-up hairstyle. Indeed, he was a hairstylist, and a barber as well, which was practical at the training camps where he sparred. He cut George Chuvalo's hair for the Floyd Patterson fight, and later on, when Cody's mother saw a rerun of the fight on television, he said to her, "See that fellow getting hit with that right cross, Ma? That's my haircut he's wearing."

As we headed north, the stops were frequent—just places where Ali felt like pulling over to the side, usually lonely places with the pines stretching away from the ditches on either side of the macadam highway, and just the faintest whir of insects in that breathless heat, so that everyone walking away from the bus seemed to talk in low voices so as not to jar the stillness too much. The sparring partners squatted in a row and chucked pebbles into the cattails in the ditches. The cooks stayed in the bus. Ali dug down with his hands to where the earth was cool, sniffing at it as it trickled through his fingers, and then he made compresses of it, and spread them on the bare arms of those around him to show them how cool it was. Back down the highway from the bus, Jimmy Ellis, who was one of his sparring mates then, found a dead snake in the weeds—a chicken snake nearly three feet long. He got ahold of it with a piece of stick and came high-stepping along, giggling, meaning to lob it at the champion, it was obvious, who watched him come for a while, and then jumped up and went down the creek bed at a great clip. Ellis kept after him,

26

but lost ground steadily because of his burden, which was difficult to handle, and he was slowed by paroxysms of laughter, practically to a standstill, and finally he looked as if he were going to fall down for laughing so hard at the champion's haste. I could see the cooks looking out the bus window, grinning and pointing. The sun rose and the heat began to shimmer off the macadam. Ali wandered back. He took a pistol out of the bus and fired it at the sky, four shots shattering the quiet, as if he were signaling for someone; the pinewoods absorbed the echoes. We heard the click of the trigger pin. "Hey, is there some more bullets?" he called out to one of the cooks in the bus. "They is some lying aroun' in the box with the croquet set."

The cook's face disappeared for a while. Then he reappeared at the window and shook his head.

Bundini was smoking a cigar. The blue smoke drifted out across the ditches. "We have no bullets for that pistol? Oh, my goodness. We is defenseless. When the Klan turns up tonight, nothin' to do but help them with the nooses."

Bundini was the most expressive character in the Ali camp; he looked not unlike the champ, and was occasionally mistaken for him, except that he had a hugely mobile face that brought his emotions close to the surface. He often launched into a sort of helter-skelter holy-roller rhetoric which must have put the Black Muslims on edge. I am not sure they accepted his close friendship with Ali easily. At the time, Bundini was married to a large Jewish woman named Rhoda Palestine; he wore the Star of David on a chain around his neck and though his religion was a hodge-podge he had put together himself (he liked to refer to God as a personal friend of his named "Shorty"), he certainly was of no mind to become a Muslim. The Muslims certainly tried. He told me that Elijah Muhammad had described him as someone who would be worth ten battalions of ministers to the movement.

Ali and Bundini had met for the first time just before the Doug

Jones fight in Madison Square Garden (which I would always remember because Ali ate some of the peanuts disgruntled fans threw at him from ringside). Bundini had been taken up to his room in a "raggedy" hotel called the American, where he found the young fighter lazing around in a clutter of clothing tossed every which way, shoes underfoot, and fight equipment hardly suitable for such a bright newcomer to the boxing scene. Bundini had asked, "Who takes care of you?" Ali said, "He do," and he pointed to a white man seated in a corner, smoking a cigar. Bundini looked over and suggested that the fighter's shoes needed polishing, and he mentioned what sort of wax should be used, and that his socks needed washing, and that the man had best *move* to care for a fighter packing people into the Garden up to the rafters and the seats where before there was nothin' there but *pigeons!* Ali listened to this in astonishment, being a Southern country boy who had never heard a white talked to in such a fashion.

"How did he react to this—this fellow in the corner?" I had asked.

"Why, he stepped right up and started in," Bundini said. "But the champ had his eye on me. The night of the fight I rode with him in the limousine to the Garden. We couldn't find a place to park, so I tol' the chauffeur to drive the car up on the sidewalk. The police came runnin' up, but I tol' them they had Cassius Clay there in the car, and if it warn't for him, they wouldn't be out there on duty. Sugar Ray, they let *him* park on the sidewalk. So they let us stay there, and that opened his eyes even mo'. He took me to the dressing room, but Angelo, he didn't know who I was, or why I was in there . . . so they made me wait outside . . . 'cept when they came out on the way to the ring I got close in behind Clay and started rubbing his neck muscles, just hanging on until we got to the ring posts. They couldn't budge me from the comer. I never seen this man box befo', but then I see Doug Jones—they call him 'Cueball'—hit him with a right hand in the fourth or fifth that just bounce him off the ropes, and when I saw him git over that, and how he bear down in the seventh round and start beatin' the man to death, he made me fall in love. I was with him from that fight on. That night, I tol' him to go to the hotel and get some Epsom salts and soak in a bath ... but he went up to a birthday party at Small's Paradise in Harlem and got sick right on the birthday cake from exhaustion and they carried him out of there stiff as a board. I said, you listen to *me* from now on."

Bundini's friends liked to say he had supplied and nurtured much of his young charge's wit, and the routines, and the rhymes; certainly he was responsible for the famous slogan: "Float like a butterfly, sting like a bee." I thought he would perform on the bus, but he seemed curiously subdued on the first part of the trip. Perhaps he was thinking of his hometown in the North of Florida where we were planning to stop so he could meet family folks he had not seen in years. When we were once again on the road, and Ali had turned the wheel over to the Muslim driver to put on his show as promised, Bundini stayed in the back of the bus—and it seemed to me he was sleeping back there.

Ali started his show with a tap dance in the door-well in front of the bus, scarcely keeping his balance in the bus's motion but doing some very fancy and noisy stepping with his big tan work boots to a musical accompaniment provided by Howard Bingham, singing "The Darktown Strutters' Ball" into his cupped hands. Jokes then followed by the dozens, the champion telling each with immense enthusiasm, usually with the punch line repeated, guffawed over, and then offered again, perhaps three or four times. "This cat had him a car, a special-built car, that do hundred eighty and which he use to agitate the cops—they come after him on this three-hundred-mile-long stretch of highway and he just *toy* with them. But this one time, this cop keep up to him. When he do hundred, the cop do the same. So he shove her up to hundred thirty, but the cop holds on. He let her out to a hundred *fifty,* and the cop is still stuck to him, the siren goin', and so this cat he shoves her down to the floor, a hundred *eighty,* and man, he don't budge an *inch* from that cop. So, he give up and pull over t' the side of the road. He say, 'You take me to jail, you do *anything* to me, but first allow me one look under the *hood* of yo' car.' So you know what he find under the hood of that car? He look under there an' he find six niggers wearing *sneakers."*

He told us he could use the word "nigger" and it was all right. "You understand?" he said. He told the joke again, as if to show us. Our laughter began to sound forced. When the show was over, he came down the aisle and visited with us. He kept us entertained.

Once, he sat down beside me and began talking about the Muslim religion—the homegrown part about the space platform manned by "men who never smile" which circles the world loaded with bombs that at the Armageddon will be dropped a mile deep into the earth and level everything. The platform was designed and set up by Allah in the person of Master Wallace Fard in 1930, and it whips through the sky at 18,000 miles per hour and can stop on a dime, revolving until the earth's collective guilt calls for the destruction to begin. Ali took out his wallet and showed me a frayed photograph of Wallace Fard, quite a pale-looking black, staring down at a book in his lap. Fard was Elijah Muhammad's instructor (Ali said that Elijah had never seen the Master asleep; he'd look through a keyhole at night and there Fard would be, working on his papers) and his "vision" was that the holocaust would come soon, in 1970, and that 154,000 Negroes would survive (almost all the figures in the Muslim mythology are exact) to get things going again. Ali had seen the platform many times, and if it wasn't cloudy out, we could see it in the night sky. Cody Jones, sitting in the next seat, nodded. He'd seen it at five AM one morning while out on roadwork with the champ—a bright light darting in the sky (I didn't dare say I thought it was probably

Venus or Jupiter)—and the champ had told him what it was, and about the bombs and the men who never smile.

I asked Ali to tell me about the Muslims' concept of the universe, and how everything had come to be. He allowed that he was not a minister, but from a long singsong explanation, almost like a litany, it was possible to piece together the following:

The black man originally inherited the moon—"people of the moon" is how they refer to themselves. There was no earth then—trillions of years ago—just the moon. Then one of the great scientists became disenchanted because he couldn't get everyone to speak the same language, and he caused, in a great rage, an enormous explosion which tore the "moon" into two parts—the larger one, the earth as it now is. There were some survivors of the explosion. The first people to inhabit the earth were all black—members of the tribe of Shabazz. But among them was an evil genius, Yakub (here Ali's voice dropped to a conspiratorial level), the devil of the Black Muslim religion. Yakub invented the white man in his laboratory, a job that took him 600 years. He is the father of the Caucasian race and was finally cast out of Paradise along with 59,999 of his inventions ... who nonetheless came to overwhelm the blacks and subjugate them. The guilt is piling up on the white, and the date of retribution is quite exact. The men who never smile will push the bombs over. The blacks will get eight to ten days' advance notice; they will be informed by pamphlets in Arabic dropped from the platform and the righteous will be told where to go to survive. I asked Ali if he expected to be one of the lucky 154,000 survivors, and he said, well, that was in the hands of someone else. He had no way of knowing. The dreadful platform came over the earth twice a week, in the night. Cody Jones nodded.

It was almost evening when we reached Sanford, Florida, which is where Bundini was reared. "Goose Hollow," he told me, "just back of Sanford, where the poor people walks on sand, and the white man, he has concrete to walk on." Bundini came and sat on an arm rest as we pulled in. He said that when Joe Louis fought, amplifiers were strung up in the pines out by one of the cabins and the folks sat around in the darkness to listen and cheer, and he remembered that a storm was whipping the pine forest during one of the broadcasts, so the words from Madison Square Garden, or wherever, were shredded away, people running around in the wild darkness trying to find out what was going on as if the words whirling off were corporeal, retrievable, like panicky chickens.

While Bundini was inside talking to his folks, the new champion sat on the porch steps, and from down the dusty street the people began cruising up to gawk. An elderly gentleman with a black stick for a cane picked his way up the path as tentatively as a heron: "Champ, you look good. You feel pretty confident?"

"He must fall," the champion said, scarcely looking up.

As usual, the children were the easiest with him, careening around corners, slowing up and casing him speculatively, and showing off as noisy as jays, and he always had a hold of the shiest of the crowd—a small girl, usually—and he'd ask her if she knew that the person talking was the champion of the whole wide world.

He motioned me over. He had an autograph book in his hand. The small boy who had given it to him leaned back against the crook of his arm. Its title page read THIS BOOK BELONGS TO COOL DADDY RODNEY THAT IS MY NAME NOT MY NUMBER. On the page opposite was written PRESIDENT KENNEDY DIED, the date, and under it, also in the block letters stark as initials in tree trunks, the name Sam Cooke, an ex-con country singer, and the date *he* had been shot. The champion riffled the pages and found all of them blank, so he went back to the beginning and signed the first ten pages. "That'll get you started," he said to the youngster.

He swung his arm open and let him loose. We set off again in the bus.

Bundini Brown said, "Let's stop and eat. I empty." No one said anything. It was dark outside, the pine forests stretching back from the road, their thin trunks showing up sticks of gray in the headlights. Four or five miles up the road the driver—he was one of the Muslims—slowed down and turned the bus into a truck stop near the Florida-Georgia border. Yulee was the name of the place. The big gas pumps with the PURE FIREBIRD gasoline emblems stood in pools of light from overhead standards, and there were a few truck trailers parked across the macadam-topped lot. The restaurant had a small neon light in the window. The champion's brother, Rachaman, said, "You're goin' watch a man face reality— that's what you're goin' to see."

Bundini climbed down from the bus and headed for the restaurant. With the bus motor switched off it was quiet outside, and warm, with the day's heat still rising from the macadam. I got out with the other journalists to go with Brown.

Ali and his group and the sparring partners left the bus, but they stayed back near the pumps.

The restaurant had a screen door that squeaked, and the people inside, six or seven couples sitting in the booths, looked up when Bundini came in. He sat down at the counter, and we flanked him on stools to either side. The waitress looked at us and put her hands together. The manager came out from behind the counter. "I'm sorry," he said. "We have a place out back. Separate facilities," he said. "The food's just the same." Through the serving window we could see two black cooks looking out. "Probably better," the manager said with a wan smile. He talked at us as if Bundini were not there. Bundini's face began working. The journalists began intimidating the manager, whipping whispered furious words at him. He stayed calm, tapping a grease stained menu against his fingertips. "In this county—Nassau County—they'd be a riot," he said simply. In the booths the people continued eating, watching over their forks as they lifted the food and put it into their mouths.

Bundini said, "The heavyweight champion of the world, and he can't get nothing to eat here." He spoke reflectively, and he spun around on his stool and stood up.

The screen door squeaked again and slapped shut. Ali stood in the room, leaning forward slightly and staring at Bundini. "You fool. What's the matter with you—you damn *fool!*" His nostrils were flared, his voice almost out of control. "I tol' you to be a Muslim. Then you don' go places where you're not wanted. You clear out of this place, nigger; you ain't wanted here, can't you *see*. They don' want you, nigger...." He reached for Bundini's denim jacket, hauled him toward him and propelled him out the door in an easy furious motion. Bundini offered no resistance. He stumbled out on the macadam as if he had been launched from a sling.

The champion rushed after him, pushing him for the bus, still vilifying him, and then Ali broke away and began leaping among the gas pumps and out across the macadam under the flat eerie light, circling among the trailers, one with a multi-thousand-dollar yacht balanced in its cradle—a lunatic backdrop for a frenzy that suddenly became as gleeful as a child's. "I'm *glad,* Bundini!" he shouted. "I'm glad! You got *showed,* Bundini, you got *showed.*"

Bundini's shoulders were hunched over and he was looking down. "Leave me alone," he kept repeating. "I'm good enough to eat here!" he shouted suddenly. "I'm a free man. If a man is a puppet, go tell Henry Ford to give him a nose and an eyeball and a new heart. God made me. Not Henry Ford."

The champion whooped with delight. He leaped high in the air and circled Bundini. "Don't you know when you not *wanted?* Face reality and dance!" he shouted.

Bundini cried back at him, "I'll be what I was, what I always been. In my heart I'm a free man. No slave chains round my heart." He escaped into the bus.

The rest of the group stood by and watched the champion, who was still capering and shouting, begin to wind down. His brother stalked about, his face lit with excitement, repeating like a litany, "A man has seen reality, seen *re-al-i-ty.*"

I went to look in through a window at the room in back. It was off the kitchen, a table with six chairs. An old magazine lay tossed in a comer. I turned back. Everyone was sitting in the bus. The tree-frog buzz began drifting across the macadam lot from the dark pinewood and swampland.

But when the Muslim driver got the bus moving again, the turmoil started afresh. Ali leaned over the top of his seat and kept railing Bundini: "Uncle Tom! Tom! Tom! Tom!" He muzzled him with a red pillow. He shouted, "This teach you a lesson, Bundini!" He leaned over and pushed down on Bundini's head. "You bow your head, Bundini."

"Leave me alone!" Bundini shouted. "My head don' belong between my knees. It's up in the stars. I'm free. I keep trying. If I find a waterhole is dry, I go on and find another."

The exchange was carried on in full volume, the rhetoric high blown, as if delivery were from a memorized morality play.

"You *shamed* yourself back there!" the champion shouted.

"*They* were ashamed," Bundini said.

"What good did that do, except to shame you?"

"That man," said Bundini, "that manager, he'll sleep on it. He may be no better, but he'll think on it, and he'll be ashamed. I dropped a little medicine in that place."

Ali whooped. "Tom! Tom! Tom!" He whacked a series of quick blows at Bundini with the red pillow. "You belong to your white master."

It got to Bundini finally, and he began to cry. His grief is unbearable to watch, his face a perfect reflection of the mask of tragedy. The champion looked at him.

"Hey, Bundini," he said softly. He mopped at Bundini's face with the red pillow—clumsy but affectionate swipes. "Leave me alone," Bundini said, barely audibly.

Ali tried to make him laugh. "Hey, Bundini," he said. "What sort of crackers was they back in that restaurant?" Bundini did not want to answer.

"I'll tell you what kind of crackers. They was not Georgia crackers; they was soda crackers. And if they're soda crackers, that makes you a graham cracker. That's what you are—a *graham cracker.*"

Bundini did not say anything.

The champion gave a great whooping laugh and belted Bundini on the top of the head with the red pillow.

Bundini's shoulders finally began shaking from laughter. "Champ," he said, "les' just train and fight—none of the other stuff. Why you make us come this way?" he said resignedly. "We could have flown over all these miserable miles."

"Don't fly over it, Bundini," Ali said, in an odd shift of mind which I remembered thinking was part of the paradox of him and made him so difficult to judge. "You fight it out, Bundini," he said, "... like your aunts and uncles have to do."

Not far down the road, Bundini, seeming to take his counsel, said again, "I'm empty. I want to eat. Lookee yonder! A Howard Johnson's coming up."

"We'll stop," the champion said grimly. He was again a Muslim. "This is Georgia, Bundini. You haven't been *showed?"* he asked incredulously.

When the bus was parked in the lot, Bundini stepped out, and this time the sparring partners, none of whom were Muslims, decided to join us, a grim group moving up the path for the restaurant, with its bright windows and the illuminated orange peaked cupola roof; behind, the Muslim contingent stood by the bus, with the champion's brother once again calling out, his voice tense with excitement, "You facing reality, Bundini—reality!"

The restaurant, which was nearly full, fell silent at our entrance; a cocktail ensemble playing "Tea For Two" over the Muzak was nearly deafening. In the booths forks and spoons were poised perhaps not surprisingly: we must have seemed a forbidding bunch; we were apprehensive, considering what had happened in Yulee, very grim and walking stiffly, eyes flicking everywhere to see where the first rebuff would come from; a formidable group, too, with the boxers part of it, tattoos showing on their broad black arms. A sheriff, if he had been sitting there, might well have stepped up and arrested us on general suspicion.

We gathered around a long table and sat down. A waitress appeared with a stack of menus. "You all look *hungry,*" she said brightly. She began passing out the menus.

Bundini began giggling. "My," he said, "no one mind if I sit at the head of the table?" The seats were rearranged, and Bundini pointed out the window at the Muslims standing by the bus. "I'm going to eat three steaks standing up so's they can see," he said.

He waved at the Muslims like a child. They looked like waifs standing out there in the dark.

Ali came in after a while, striding through the restaurant, the people watching him, and those with children getting ready to push them up for autographs.

"What you doin' here?" Bundini said smugly. "This place only for integrators. Soda *and* graham crackers."

The champion smiled at him and sat down. He had his meal, and when his coffee came, he said, "Bundini, I'm goin' to integrate the coffee." He poured some cream into it. "When it's black, it's strong."

Bundini shook his head. The two were smiling at each other. "Champ," said Bundini once again, "les' just train and fight—none of the other stuff."

The Roots
of Combat

Bruce Thomas

Although Bruce Lee was grounded in the school of wing chun," wrote Doug Palmer, "every time I met him he had expanded the style to include not only the corpus of what had gone before but a whole new dimension that magnified the effectiveness and universality of his own 'school.' This was not mere technique. Jeet kune do transcended style. Style was too limiting, a straitjacket, in Bruce's view. Jeet kune do was an approach, a philosophy, a Way."

This "way" was summarized in the words of a sign which hung on the wall of Bruce's school. It read: "The truth in combat is different for each individual. Research your own experiences for the truth. Absorb what is useful. Reject what is useless. Add what is specifically your own. Man, the creating individual, is more important than any style or system."

During the 1970s a lot of martial artists, believing that they were following Bruce Lee's philosophy, cast aside their systems only to discover that with no structure they were virtually useless.

They had moved away from being blindly traditional only to become blindly nontraditional.

The philosophy of jeet kune do also prompted many martial artists to take a more eclectic approach. But again, if the individual is not *grounded* in one form to begin with, then this approach will fall well short of what Bruce Lee intended. To "absorb what is useful" does not mean simply to select, assemble, and accumulate techniques from many different styles, thinking that your new hybrid will have the best of everything. To absorb what is useful first requires a "body feel" that you can work from.

"Bruce thought you could teach a discipline without discipline," said William Cheung. "This is not possible. However much people venerate Bruce Lee, this part of his thinking is mistaken. You *do* need forms: otherwise, how can you break away when you have nothing to break away from? What is jeet kune do but an amalgam of styles which is claiming to be free of styles? I told Bruce this. I say that we are born without knowledge. We have to acquire it first before we can be free of it."

These remarks are echoed by Dan Inosanto: "Bruce didn't like anything organized and, according to him, jeet kune do was not to have a blueprint; that was his whole philosophy at the time. I said, 'Well, you've got to start from some place; even a child has to be taught something before he can express freedom.'"

Despite William Cheung and Dan Inosanto's assertions, we should remind ourselves that Bruce practiced the wing chun forms regularly long after he had moved to America. Film of Bruce shot in Oakland shows him performing the *sil lum tao*; his movements are disciplined, refined, and precise. On his return visits to Hong Kong, Bruce would seek out Yip Man specifically to complete his learning of the wooden dummy form, which he also practiced intensively.

As Dan Inosanto said earlier, Bruce would sometimes point himself in one direction and his students in another. Bruce never taught forms to any of his students; but he preferred to teach people who had already been through *formal* training since they could then appreciate what he had to offer. Bruce believed that novices needed to learn forms but that, once a certain level of understanding was reached, the martial artist could go outside of fixed boundaries to where the true expression of the art is found.

A martial artist can't begin from no stance, no form, or no technique, just as a musician cannot go straight to being a virtuoso. Each must learn the fundamentals and forms of music or fighting out of which he can progress, and which he can then use as a basis for improvisation and creativity. Only then can he start "rejecting what is useless" by throwing away what doesn't work for him personally. But, here again, self-knowledge must enter the equation—not being able to perform a technique successfully doesn't automatically mean that the technique is useless!

It is clear that Bruce Lee began his martial artistry with wing chun and then went on to study other methods. Yet this was not so much a process of adding and accumulating techniques, but of *incorporating* them into simple principles.

Neither does to "add what is specifically your own" mean adding personal embellishments to the art. For example: none of us now drive the way we originally learned in order to pass our driving test. Through experience we have all made our own personal modifications, so that we can now steer with one hand and operate the radio with the other instead of having to steer with both hands.

What does Bruce Lee mean by "Man the creating individual is more important than any established style or system"? The important distinction here is between "style" and "individual style." All boxers, for example, have the same basic style. But Muhammad Ali did not fight like Joe Frazier; modern boxers fight differently from the early champions. In the same way, Western martial artists have a more powerful build while Asian martial artists are lighter and faster. In going beyond basic technical skills, the fighter attempts to get the best from his or her own particular attributes—temperament, speed, power, strategic awareness, and so on. Again, the key factor is in actually *doing* it so that it is not merely theoretical knowledge but understanding based on experience.

Anyone who attempts to define jeet kune do runs the risk of being like those in the fable of the blind men attempting to describe an elephant; one felt the tail and thought the elephant was like a snake; another felt its leg and thought it was like a tree, and so on. Human nature, being what it is, means that each person can relate only to what he or she already understands. Naturally a wing chun practitioner will see the foundation of Bruce's art as wing chun.

Before he met Bruce Lee, Jim Kelly had already applied the principles of jeet kune do through his individual approach to karate, resulting in a different understanding to that of most of its practitioners. Bruce recognized what Kelly had done and paid him the ultimate compliment by not choreographing Kelly's fights in *Enter the Dragon,* telling Kelly that he understood his own art and should do what he wanted.

Conversely, anyone approaching jeet kune do nowadays might be forgiven for thinking that it is a Filipino martial art, now that through Dan Inosanto it has become closely associated with his own preferred art of kali.

The real meaning of jeet kune do, after a sufficient level of technical ability has been reached, is to use it as a means of self-discovery and self-expression. Jeet kune do does not apply to those of us who are learning the basic skill; it is a concept or philosophy that implies a level of mastery, and, consequently, of self-mastery.

In this way, a kali practitioner, a *karateka,* or a wing chun exponent may also evolve out of the techniques and forms of his or her style, without dispensing with technique or losing form. And if they choose to, they may then call their mastery, "Jeet Kune Do," or "Body, Mind, and Spirit," or whatever they please.

Bob Wall comments:

> Bruce challenged the foundations of the traditional martial arts by saying that the martial arts should be an extension of yourself. Before he came along, the Koreans thought that their style was the best, the Japanese thought that their style was the best. —Bruce said that a punch in the mouth was a punch in the mouth.

As student Pete Jacobs put it when asked what Bruce Lee's favorite move was, he replied, "Hitting you!"

"My truth is not your truth," said Bruce Lee. What worked for Bruce didn't necessarily work for Jim Kelly or Dan Inosanto, nor for Joe Lewis.

"I never believed in that 'power-side forward' stuff," says Lewis. Yet in declining to adopt Bruce Lee's recommended stance, Lewis is actually embracing jeet kune do's core philosophy. From his work with Bruce, Joe Lewis absorbed what was useful and freed himself from the constraints of classical karate.

As a consequence, within his first year of training with Bruce Lee, Joe Lewis became unassailable in tournament competition. Ten of the greatest karate men of the day fought Lewis, and all ten were knocked out before the end of the second round. Joe Lewis was the most successful competition fighter among Bruce's "students."

It was Bruce who suggested to Joe Lewis that he try using boxing techniques in karate; he also showed him the use of the "angular attack," a principle found in wing chun. Further encouraged by Bruce to try out more realistic forms of combat, Lewis became one of the pioneers of the sport of full-contact karate in the early 1970s. In effect, Bruce was devising strategies, and Lewis was testing them out in the ring.

The tae kwon do master Jhoon Rhee, who respected both Bruce's skills and his "rebellious" attitude, devised and introduced the "Safe-T" equipment that was first utilized in the World Professional Karate Championships in 1974. Bruce's training methods were made public by Lewis's competition appearances, combined with the use of Jhoon Rhee's protective equipment. In this way, Bruce Lee was at the root of the growth of martial arts into a competition sport in the West. In its infancy, modern American kickboxing was nothing less than applied jeet kune do.

Joe Lewis and his student Tom Tannenbaum (the producer of *Longstreet* who had moved on to become head of Universal TV) were instrumental in producing a ninety-minute special out of the 1974 championships. This event established the sport of full-contact karate.

As Bruce Lee himself never fought in tournament competition, the question of how he would have fared is open to debate. Jim Kelly, for one, has suggested that many of the martial artists he did spar against have not revealed all that they know because they are protecting their own and each others' reputations. Richard Bustillo and a Los Angeles policeman were both present at a sparring session between Bruce and Chuck Norris in which the karate champion was left "red-faced."

Howard Williams adds that Bruce wasn't tempted to involve jeet kune do in tournament sport because he didn't hold with rules in combat, and that both Bruce's methods and attitude would have led to disqualification.

Yet Bruce's influence continued to be felt in the ring. In his June 1982 interview for *Playboy,* boxing champion Sugar Ray Leonard said:

One of the guys who influenced me wasn't a boxer. I always loved the catlike reflexes and the artistry of Bruce Lee and I wanted to do in boxing what he was able to do in karate [sic]. I started watching his movies before he became really popular in *Enter the*

Dragon and I patterned myself after a lot of his ways. Lee was an artist and like him I try to go beyond the fundamentals of my sport.

Bruce Lee always regretted that he came up with the expression jeet kune do, rightly anticipating that it would suffer the fate of being turned from a fluid concept into a fixed or "classical" system. Given Bruce's feelings about the classical martial arts, it is ironic that in 1981, the Kuosho Federation of the Republic of China made jeet kune do a legitimate martial art whose official hierarchy consists of "elders" like Dan Inosanto and Taky Kimura and their "descendants" such as Tim Tackett.

Although Taky Kimura still teaches a small private class in what he calls *"jun fan gung fu,"* it is obvious that Bruce's art has taken more than a few twists and turns since the day he told Taky, "Get a nondescript little place and work out there; have a good time, develop strong friendships and a good philosophy."

Bruce also knew that martial arts suffer the same fate as religions. Now there are already several versions of "jeet kune do" being presented. There are those who teach the screen version of Bruce's fighting and call it "jeet kune do." There are those teaching "classic jeet kune do" who list the ten pointers that distinguish the "real" art. There are some who invent a hybrid style and teach whatever they like, then label it "jeet kune do." Almost beyond belief are the so-called "jeet kune do" institutes that offer home study correspondence courses, complete with diplomas, in streetfighting!

Even Dan Inosanto has been accused of misleading people. In recent years, Howard Williams has presented himself as a no-nonsense streetfighter, explaining that he considers jeet kune do to be the "original" art that Bruce taught in Oakland and adding that it cannot be mixed with other styles like kali. "People think that they can mix up these things, but it's like oil and water: you can shake them up and they look like they've mixed, but if you leave them a while they begin to separate out."

Jeet kune do instructor Richard Bustillo asks, "But what does 'original' mean? Is that original from Bruce's days in Hong Kong, Seattle, Oakland, or Los Angeles? Anything that Bruce Lee might be teaching today would certainly have evolved to incorporate new energies."

In teaching "jeet kune do" many of Bruce's descendants begin from points at which he himself arrived only after ten, twelve, or fifteen years of hard-won experience. None had the opportunity to study or practice the vital foundation which permitted his later growth. Bruce's jeet kune do was the blossom on a tree with very deep roots.

Bruce Lee continued to practice the wing chun forms long after he had left Hong Kong. It was only because the awareness they developed had become so embodied in him—so that he didn't merely "know" it, but *was* it—that he could later use that body feel to be free enough to bend the rules.

It is pointless to make an empty imitation of Bruce Lee's freedom. One must have first practiced clearly-defined patterns. Creativity emerges from the limits of form—from having only seven colors, only twelve notes, or only two arms and two legs to work with. "If there were people with four arms and four legs," said Bruce, "then there would be another way of fighting." There would also be other forms of music!

To wander "in a circle with no circumference" is not to be free but rather to be lost. Perhaps what Bruce Lee meant to say is that the (martial) artist must learn how to function in a small, well-defined circle, until it may eventually be enlarged a little at a time until it *seemingly* has no edges.

"Keep blasting, pushing, and flowing," Bruce urged. But this kind of spirited flow has to be understood in its right relationship to form. For example, there is not a limitless number of ways to block a kick with one's hand; there are only a few ways to do this safely and effectively—and all are based on the laws of anatomy (human form) and physics (the flow of energy). One cannot expect simply to "flow" instinctively into the right move. The opposite is true; we have to practice the right move many, many times before we can flow into it.

We can only learn to do what we want to do by repeatedly doing it, by making all the required neuromuscular connections, or, if you prefer, by opening the right energy channels. But the key to learning by repetition is never to allow it to become stale or mechanical but to practice with *awareness*. In this way, we never "do" the forms or "do" techniques, but search within them.

This process reveals the truth in its own time. Like the growth of a garden, it is not something that can be constructed but must unfold from the inside, from the ground of its own being. The body itself teaches you as it learns.

This process allows a continual refinement and while it may seem to contradict the previous paragraph, it may also be likened to the sculptor who chips away at a block of stone to reveal the "form" within. In this way, any *inessential* emotional tension, physical stiffness, or mental distraction may gradually be chipped away to reveal the master within.

In short, the truth unfolds from the inside, while what is unnecessary falls away.

Only this, and not empty imitation, leads to the development of economical and efficient movements and the subsequent speed and power that they bring. Practicing with good form is the principal means for generating, and opening up, the channels for the internal energy of *ch'i*.

Bruce Lee explained the difference between "having no form" and having "no form." *Having no form* (at all) means simply being slap-happy and incompetent. Having *no* (fixed) *form* means that one is not restricted by form but is able to use it without being tied to it. Combined with another useful habit, awareness of fighting range, all of these elements are then introduced into training. The pressure is gradually increased as the fighter attempts to *hold form* and not dissolve into useless human reaction. Only then can there be any possibility of the "tools striking on their own" when faced with a serious attack. *All of this is precisely what should happen in the practice of sticking hands.*

The most valuable and, I believe, indispensable tool that Bruce Lee had for understanding the roots of combat came from his grounding in the practice of sticking hands, *chi sao,* which develops the awareness that allowed him to flow into spontaneous expression.

Bruce could say that he was "no style, but all styles" because the reflexes that he'd acquired from sticking hands allowed him to automatically match any attack with the appropriate counter. In this way, *his* technique was the result of his opponent's technique. "You don't know what I'm going to do," Bruce would say. *Neither did Bruce*—until it had happened!

But just as Bruce did not teach his students any forms, he hadn't the time to spend years on the intensive one-to-one teaching of sticking hands. Yet the fact that Bruce Lee considered *chi sao* the cornerstone of his art is evident in the photographs showing him teaching it to Van Williams during a publicity shoot for *The Green Hornet.* Years later, in similar situations, he was also photographed doing the same thing with James Franciscus, and also with John Saxon on the set of *Enter the Dragon.*

The practice of *chi sao* serves to develop the "contact reflex" and the experience of "forward pressure" which, at their fullest expression, extend far beyond trapping range and even far beyond the physical realm to allow the instantaneous understanding of the energy and intention of the opponent while eliciting the automatic response to solve any problem being set by him. However, it should also be made clear that this wing chun-based exercise is only truly effective when allied to the strategic use of footwork. Bruce Lee discovered this, just as Derek Jones did, though each of them solved the problem in his own particular way.

Nowadays, the practice of sticking hands is almost universally misunderstood. Most people realize only a fraction of its potential by practicing fragments of it as set moves often involving "wrong" positions. Properly understood, sticking hands is a continuously flowing exercise that primarily allows one to "hold form" and search within the interplay of energy.

Practiced hour after hour and day after day as the basis of sparring, *chi sao* is performed as a kind of moving meditation that fuses with the practice of the form and techniques. *This* is the central core which allows an organic understanding of the roots of combat, and which also allows the martial artist to transcend all styles.

In music, as in dancing and fighting, there is a continual flow of movement. Bruce Lee was aware of their relationship and would spend many hours listening to Indian music on headphones because he wanted to absorb its improvised melodies and fluid rhythmic patterns.

In my own experience, learning a martial art has parallels with learning to play music. The musical group with which I play has attempted to bring together rock, pop, country, soul, blues, and reggae while retaining a recognizable style. Yet in order to be able to cross those musical boundaries freely, I had first spent many years rooting my technique in fundamental skills such as rhythm and timing (and playing the right notes!) by copying simple riffs from my favorite R&B records. Bruce Lee rooted his skills in wing chun before he integrated fencing, boxing, kickboxing, wrestling, and jiujutsu.

Even if at times it looked as if Bruce Lee was teaching music that only he could play, what he hoped to do was to teach people enough from which they would also be able to improvise, rather than merely play "set" pieces.

Yet, whether a musician leans toward playing jazz, classical, or country music, the same forms—the same scales, chord structures, harmony, and dissonance—apply to all. Having said that, one only has to listen to the attempts of the majority of classically-trained musicians to improvise "feel" music, like rock or blues, to realize the disadvantages of a purely formal training. So one must also begin with a certain amount of freedom. One musician may excel in one form of expression, another may take a different road; if they both have talent and work on it, both will get to where they want to go.

Playing music, like practicing a martial art, may serve many purposes: to make money, to show off, to get laid, to terrify, or to heal. It can be used by the narcissistic personality for its own ends; or it can be a vehicle for spirit and for truth.

In this way, awareness may combine with intention to form the basis not only of martial arts mastery but of the mastery of any form of art or means of expression. And it may also be the key to all forms of enlightenment—whether this is called "philosophical insight," "spiritual revelation," "liberation," or "mastery."

From Fatso to Breakfalls: Learning to Accept My Body

Carol A. Wiley

In the seventh grade I sat and watched the teacher weigh and measure the height of the other students, then send them out to recess. I stepped on the scale: 5'7" and 214 pounds. The teacher had not wanted to embarrass me in front of the other children, yet her disapproval was obvious. All my life I had heard from adults that I should lose weight. All my life I had endured the taunts of other children: "Fatso." "Titanic." Two more years of this pressure and, at fourteen, I began fifteen years of yo-yo dieting and trying to fit my body into a package deemed acceptable by society.

I lost fifty pounds when I was fourteen, which met with everyone's approval, but I was a shy teenager, uncomfortable with people, and losing weight didn't give me the popularity I wanted. Yet out of this loneliness grew an interest that has become central to the development of both my body and my mind. Movies and books were my companions. I saw nearly every appropriately rated movie that showed at the one theater in town, which included many of the Bruce Lee and other kung fu movies popular in the early 1970s. The movement I saw on the screen fascinated me, and I longed to try it for myself.

No one taught the martial arts in my small town, so I enrolled in a kung fu class in a nearby city, but getting to class was difficult and I dropped it after about two weeks. I attempted a karate class during my first year of college. That also lasted about two weeks. In both classes I was reticent and self-conscious, and the instructors did nothing to encourage me. They even seemed amused I was there: I was a woman, I was big, I was uncoordinated.

But my desire to study the martial arts didn't disappear. During my senior year of college, 1979, I started a karate class and stuck with it. Although still self-conscious, I felt less out of place in this physical education class where I blended in with about twenty-five other uncoordinated people. I learned techniques as well as anyone else, sometimes better, and I was soon hooked.

I finished college, moved to a new city, and found a tae kwon do class. I started the class with ten other people; after a year I was the only one still training; after two-and-a-half years I was the senior student; after three-and-a-half years I received my black belt. My coordination and strength improved tremendously, as did my concentration and focus. Yet I still fought my body: during that time I weighed between 180 and 190 pounds and was constantly berating myself and trying to lose weight.

A few months after receiving my black belt I moved to another city and returned to school for a master's degree. I trained at the university tae kwon do club for three months, but didn't like the instructor's approach. To try something different, I trained in arnis (Filipino stick-fighting) for six months, but then that was no longer available. For sixteen months I did not train. I kept putting it off. I had gained about forty pounds. I thought this weight would prevent me from training the way I used to, and I was embarrassed to go into a school and say I had a black belt. But my desire to train was greater than my doubts, and I started training again in tae kwon do in 1986.

I didn't lose weight, which surprised and bothered me at first, but as I saw my body respond to the physical activity, I thought less about my weight. Because the tae kwon do school had only been open a few months, I soon became the senior student and assistant instructor. In 1988 I received my second degree black belt.

When the tae kwon do school closed in 1989, I decided to expand my martial arts experience and began training in aikido. My proficiency with the linear movements of tae kwon do did not translate immediately to the circular and spiral movements of aikido. I also had to learn to fall and roll, which was a frustrating and sometimes painful experience. Aikido classes did not give me the exhilarated feeling that tae kwon do classes usually had. More often, I felt depressed and frustrated.

The difficult transition almost led me to quit aikido and find a tae kwon do school. I wasn't sure why I stuck with aikido, but somehow I felt there was something to learn. After a year I enjoyed the movement of aikido, felt less awkward, and had begun to understand aikido's approach. Then came a big moment: I did my first breakfall. A breakfall is like a half-flip, a roll without any contact with the mat. I never thought my body could fly through the air like that.

The physical benefits of the martial arts are obvious: improved coordination, strength, and endurance. But the mental benefits are more important: the true martial artist knows that the mind is a more powerful weapon than the body. Training develops focus, concentration, awareness, and self-confidence. These elements are important not only in a self-defense situation but also in all other areas of life.

When people ask why I train in the martial arts, I often say that I train for the satisfaction of doing something physically useful and mentally challenging. But deep inside I know that I cannot not train, for training fills an important part of my being. When things are right, it's pure pleasure. Of course, there's also the exhaustion and occasional injury. And sometimes nothing seems to work, and it's pure frustration. Through it all I feel something deep in my being that I know is more important than the momentary pleasure or pain.

The martial arts have been important in helping me accept my body. If I can do all this, what's so great about being thin? A few years ago I stopped dieting, tentatively at first, but with increasing conviction, especially as I read more about the dangers of yo-yo dieting. I eat nutritiously and let my weight find its own level, a level that has proven to be neither the lightest nor heaviest I have been as an adult. Weight is now a much less important part of my life, but the martial arts remain important, training my body, my mind, and my spirit.

Jôgo Bonito:
Brief Anatomy
of Capoeira

Ben Downing

S alve 300 anos de Zumbi," proclaimed the banner above the Cantina da Lua in Pelourinho, the colonial center of Salvador, Brazil, when I arrived in November 1995. As Pelourinho means "whipping post," in reference to the slaves who were punished there, it seemed trenchantly, pleasingly ironic that the man whom the banner urged me to hail, Zumbi of Palmares, had flouted Lusitanian authority like few others. When Zumbi was finally ambushed by government troops on November 20, 1695 and his severed head put on display in the city of Recife, it brought to an emphatic, grisly end the remarkable "kingdom" of Palmares, whose last ruler Zumbi had been. Lasting most of the seventeenth century, Palmares was the largest and hardiest of the *quilombos,* communities of runaway slaves scattered around the Brazilian hinterland. The historical record is sketchy and sporadic at best, but the *quilombos* appear to have defended themselves with a blend of guerrilla stealth and what armor they could steal or, in some cases, forge. They may also—although this is probably a matter of wishful speculation—have used a homebrewed martial art called capoeira; legend has it that Zumbi himself was a master of the form.

The tercentenary seemed a promising coincidence, since the capoeira association I had come to study with is called Grupo Palmares. I had already spent two years with the New York outpost of Palmares, and was drawn to Bahia (the state of which Salvador is the capital) in part to experience capoeira in its native habitat, and in part out of curiosity about the rich, Afro-Brazilian fusion that produced it. As early as the nineteenth century, Sir Richard Burton found that *baianos,* as residents of Bahia are called, estimated themselves "the *crème* of the Brazilian *crème,*" and the same holds true today, minus the snootiness that phrase implies: they are justly proud of their culture, more uniquely Brazilian than that of the rather Europeanized southern states. Bahia has its own distinctive cuisine; in *candomblé* its own vibrant cult; a profusion of musical styles, including *afoxé* and the cobblestone-pounding *blocos,* thunderous percussion armies of which Olodum (thanks to Paul Simon and soon, alas, to Michael Jackson in his forthcoming video, shot in Salvador and Rio) is only the most famous among hundreds; and, of course, it has capoeira.

When talking about capoeira to the unfamiliar, the first problem is simply defining it; every non-Brazilian practitioner, eager to share his exotic hobby, must struggle to do so. My own explanations usually conclude with the frustrated assertion that you just have to see for yourself. For despite my earlier labeling of capoeira as a martial art, combat accounts for only part of the puzzle. Dance is certainly another, and capoeira often gets tagged as a sort of "fighting dance." What casual observers often miss, however, is the crucial extent to which capoeira thinks of itself as a game; the Portuguese verb used for the activity of "doing" capoeira is *jogar,* "to play." The best one-line encapsulation I've come up with so far—although I resist such summaries, since capoeira is decidedly *not* a hybrid form—claims capoeira to be a fight within a dance within a game, each definition circumscribing the previous one like a nest of Russian dolls. I might also trace, more faintly, an outer shell of ritual surrounding it all, because the game unfolds in a charged, almost formal atmosphere governed by quirky laws and bewildering etiquette.

Capoeira's equivalent of high mass is the *roda*—literally, "wheel" or "circle." A *roda* happens whenever and wherever a congregation of *capoeiristas,* from a bare-bones five or six to dozens, accumulates. It may be indoors, around the painted circle on an academy floor, or in a park or plaza, where a perimeter of spectators delineates the arena. There are regular, scheduled *rodas,* such as those outside the Mercado Modelo, a large market in Salvador, and spontaneous tourneys at the beach. Some are restricted to members of the host academy, others open to *capoeiristas*-errant. Players like to drop in on each other's *rodas* and *batizados*—"baptisms," at which new players are initiated and older ones promoted, and which feature epic *rodas*—attract nomad *capoeiristas* from thousands of miles around; it is now considered de rigeur for a U.S. academy to fly in a bevy of Brazilian hotshots for its annual *batizado.*

Besides the players themselves, the other essential ingredient for a *roda* is music. I will have more to say about capoeira music later, but for now suffice it to picture a *bateria* of two to ten percussion instruments, led by the bow-shaped *berimbau,* arranged around one arc of the circle. To open the *roda,* the *berimbau* kicks up a *toque* (literally, "touch," but meaning "rhythm"), usually a slow one. Once the rest of the instruments have joined in, someone—often the senior *mestre* ("master") present—bellows *"Iê!"* and then sings a solo known as a *ladainha* ("litany"), a eulogy to, typically, capoeira itself, the *berimbau,* or the foxiness of the girls on such-and-such a *baiano* island (PC has yet to purge capoeira lyrics). The *ladainha* may be chosen from a traditional repertoire or vamped on the spot, yet it always blends into the *chula,* where the soloist in quick succession praises, among other things, his God and his own *mestre,* with the chorus swelling in, sudden and rousing, to echo him.

Meanwhile, a pair of *capoeiristas* will be squatting at the foot of the lead *berimbau,* waiting to play. During the *chula,* they may unleash a string of grand, appreciative gestures upward to God, laterally to the *bateria,* and across to each other. In preparation, they may also cross themselves and make arcane, talismanic finger-squiggles on the floor. When the *chula* is finished and everything thoroughly invoked, extolled, and blessed, the *bateria* settles into a series of *corridos* (a kind of call-response song) sung by anyone inspired to, the *berimbau* briefly dips between the two players, they shake hands, and the game begins.

Despite a common body of tactics known and used by all *capoeiristas,* what follows is purely improvisational. In time to the casual beat, the players will move out into the *roda* with *aús* (modified cartwheels), *meia-luas* ("half-moons," low circular kicks), various techniques for skittering smoothly across the floor, and, most importantly, the *ginga* ("swing"), a sort of bob-and-weave dance step from which the other movements radiate, and to which they always return. Most *golpes* ("strikes") in capoeira are launched with the feet or head; when one player proffers a kick or head-butt, the other uses an *esquiva* ("avoidance") to politely decline it, and then makes his rebuttal. The better the *capoeiristas,* the less distinction there will be between attack and defense. Blocks are used only as a last resort, and are shunned as gumming up the natural fluidity of play. They are, however, rarely needed anyway, since the predominant ethic in capoeira is to "show" attacks, not complete them; it takes far more skill to freeze your kick a hair's breadth from your opponent's face than actually to drive it home.

Although there are numerous *rasteiras* ("trips"), takedowns, and other contact—involving maneuvers in the capoeira vocabulary, experienced players can—and often do—conduct an elaborate, sinuous, largely upside-down game inches away from each other, shadowing but never touching. They may also execute the game as if trapped under a waist-high glass ceiling. This happens particularly at the beginning of the *roda,* when the *toque* is unhurried and the play nearly meditative; some *rodas* are played out largely within three feet of the floor. At others, though, the music gradually accelerates and the *capoeiristas,* as if recapitulating our vertical evolution, come up off the ground, mix in more *golpes* and *floreios* (acrobatic "flourishes"), and play faster.

One of capoeira's many ambiguities is to be a game without absolute rules, objectives, or winners and losers. Sweeping your opponent's feet out from under him or rudely booting him, *à la* sumo, from the *roda,* are both perfectly fair play and the closest capoeira comes to tabular scoring. Less quantifiably, players jockey for control of the match, for the prestige of cramping the other guy's style rather than having his lorded over you; one wants to impose, not be imposed upon, to be the hemmer-in and not the hemmed. But most of all, capoeira is, as T.S. Eliot might say, autotelic: the point of the game is to play the game. It is for the two *capoeiristas* involved to make of it what they will, and in each bout they tacitly set, by gesture, the mood and relative truculence of their encounter. They may work almost as a team, with the shared goal of staging an elegant, kinetic tableau—or just looking stupendously cool. Then again, they may, on rare occasion, go at each other with mad-dog viciousness, in which case the aim becomes the humiliation, or even injury, of the other player. To me, the best matches strike a happy balance between competition and cooperation, the *capoeiristas* pushing each other to Himalayan levels of athleticism and ingenuity.

When a player decides he's had enough, he will return to the foot of the *berimbau,* shake hands with his partner, exit the *roda,* and take over an instrument in the *bateria* so someone else can play. Also, a third player may sidle into the *roda* to *comprar o jôgo* ("buy the game"), rather like cutting in on a waltz. If the presiding *mestre* thinks two players have overstayed their welcome or are misbehaving, he may call them back with a repeated note on his lowered *berimbau,* dress them down, and either let them resume play or send them temporarily packing. Barring any significant outbreak of violence, a *roda* can carry on in this manner for hours on end, usually concluding at a fever pitch—the *bateria* firing away, the players a blurred knot of Tasmanian devils, the air sweaty and electric.

Such, then, is the basic format of the contemporary *roda de capoeira.* Yet how the game began and evolved down the years remains an issue of heated, murky, ill-substantiated, and often tendentious debate. In an interesting parallel to U.S. Afrocentrism, some Brazilian blacks, perhaps anxious at white encroachments on their heritage, have insisted that capoeira was brought over, wholesale and intact, from across the Atlantic; to stress this connection, one of the two major styles calls itself *capoeira Angola.* That capoeira is at least partially a product of the African Diaspora seems indisputable. The language of capoeira is riddled with Bantu words, and scholars like Robert Francis Thompson, the Yale anthropologist, have painstakingly documented the tantalizing affinities between capoeira and, on the one hand, African practices like the *n'golo* or "zebra dance" of southern Angola, and such New World self-defense systems as Venezuelan *broma,* Martiniquean *ladjá,* and Cuban *maní* on the other.

Even the etymology of capoeira has been vigorously, and quite fruitlessly, contested; neither of the two leading derivations— from another meaning of the word capoeira, "secondary growth," and from *capão,* "capon"—makes a great deal of sense or sheds useful light on the game's origins. Unfortunately, much of what passes for capoeira "scholarship" proceeds with a blithe disregard for evidence, sustained more by enthusiasm than rigor. At a recent *batizado* in New York, for example, the audience was reverently informed that capoeira is "five hundred years old"—a nice, rounded, venerable figure to be sure, but utterly random and baseless.

As previously mentioned, one of the game's enduring myths (all of which may or may not be true) links capoeira to Zumbi and the *quilombos;* another has capoeira being born in the *senzalas,* the slave quarters attached to plantations. According to this theory, the game's preponderance of foot and head attacks is due to the fact that the slaves' hands were often manacled. It can explain, moreover, the relative reticence of capoeira's martial aspect as a necessary bit of hoodwinking: colonial whitey would see only an odd dance—"a bunch of Third World freaks jumping around," as a friend's skeptical father once scoffed—and overlook the potential menace to him tucked within the moves. Since the slaves couldn't train at their martial art openly, the plausible thinking goes, they stashed it behind a bright facade of harmlessness.

What portion of capoeira was smuggled over from Africa, whether it arose in the *quilombos* or *senzalas,* and when it cohered into a distinct practice with a name, will probably never be established to any degree of certainty. In the absence of definitive data, it is perhaps best merely to observe that it took shape under the particular pressures of Brazilian slavery, in the same sense that the blues emerged from the *norteamericano* version of the "peculiar institution," as the euphemism went. Capoeira considers itself to be a slave art, and proudly so; a leading current association is called, in memory of the game's shackled roots, Grupo Senzala. Even today, many players—especially poorer, darker-skinned ones—find in capoeira a jubilant metaphor for defiance and liberation.

Ironically enough, the first *capoeirista* to be brought to public attention was neither a slave nor even a *baiano,* but a Portuguese lieutenant known as Amotinado ("rebel" or "mutineer"), feared bodyguard to viceroy Marquis de Lavradio. In a series of articles written around 1770, the Rio journalist Manoel de Macedo detailed the unpeaceful escapades of this scrapper, who apparently used capoeira, among other things, to protect his charge during the viceroy's infamous, all-night dalliances. Capoeira next surfaces in officialdom around 1810, when the first commander of the Royal Guard in Rio, Major Nunes Vidigal, himself reputedly an ace *capoeirista*, began cracking down on his fellow adepts; a common charge pressed by the police at the time was for the street crime of capoeira. To avoid attack or arrest, *capoeiras* (as they were then called) would play a special warning *toque* on the *berimbau*, known as *cavalaria*, to disperse a *roda* before the oncoming gendarmerie.

In fact, the word capoeira was long a synonym not only for the players themselves, but for low-life generally. Brazilian Portuguese is, not surprisingly, affluent with words for hooliganism and chicanery, and even quite recent Portuguese-English dictionaries will list "ruffian" as one of the meanings of capoeira. Although the game has become hugely more respectable, some Brazilians remain wary of its devotees; one English student of mine in Salvador, a well-to-do dentist, frequently cautioned me against the treacherous and underhanded ways of *capoeiristas*.

So strong was the stigma attached to capoeira during the nineteenth century that a federal statute was enacted against it in 1890. The novelist Machado de Assis begged to differ in 1893, contending that the *capoeiristas'* skills could potentially be harnessed to good civic effect. As it happens, this notion had already been tried in 1828, when razor-wielding players were turned loose on rioting German and Irish mercenaries in Rio, much to the soldiers' bodily distress. And it was tested again during the Brazilian war with Paraguay (1865–70), in which *capoeiristas* were reported on the front lines. Except for these occasional episodes of cynical state sponsorship, however, the art was vehemently discouraged through the early decades of our own century, and seems to have been driven back from the rest of Brazil into Bahia. Jorge Amado gives us a thumbnail portrait of how capoeira looked at the time in the most celebrated of Brazilian novels, *Gabriela, Clove and Cinnamon,* set in Ilheus, Bahia, circa 1925:

> On Sunday afternoons, Negroes and mulattos gathered in the yard behind the house to watch and engage in capoeira, the curious fight contest of the region. Sete Voltas played the one-string instrument that usually accompanies capoeira and sang:
>
> > "Comrade in battle
> > Together let's wander
> > The wide world over.
> > Comrade, ah, comrade!"
>
> He handed the instrument to Nilo and entered the capoeira ring. With cartwheels and sudden thrusts of the feet and elbows, all in rhythm, he outpointed his opponents and remained alone and victorious on the field of battle.

It was, appropriately, in Bahia that the turning point came in the 1930s, during the regime of Getúlio Vargas, a president with such consummate flair for the melodramatic that he committed suicide while in office. When Mestre Bimba opened the first capoeira academy in Salvador, the game began its migration from the squalid alleys and docks—it was popular with *stevedores*—to household acceptability; the school was recognized by the government in 1937. Bimba called his version *capoeira regional* (to emphasize what he took to be the game's "regional," *baiano* origins), and taught it as a self-defense system, complete with a diploma at the end. Shortly thereafter, Mestre Pastinha followed suit, but offered instead a more traditional brand of capoeira, which he christened *Angola.*

In photographs, Bimba looms out as a massive, solemn, somehow tragic-looking figure; he would make an excellent Othello.

Pastinha, meanwhile, is the very image of a Puck: tiny, bright-eyed, prankish. And to a degree, their bearings are emblematic of the orders they founded. For *regional,* as one general style of capoeira continues to be known, is rougher, faster, more martial and no-nonsense than *Angola,* which stresses strategy and cunning over brute force, the game and the music over the fight, and the goofball over the grunt. Students of *regional* favor wearing only plain, white pants like the slaves in the *senzalas,* whereas *Angoleiros* are given to natty khakis, crisp, button-down shirts, and shoes. (With both schools, however, it is a point of pride to keep one's clothes clean, as visible proof that no one has dropped you to the floor or put his skanky feet on you.)

Naturally, these differences have sparked endless, and often tiresome, factional squabbling about who represents the "true" capoeira; *regional* players tend to lambaste *Angoleiros* as floppy, geriatric floor-crawlers, who in turn pooh-pooh their counterparts as humor—and artless robots. *Capoeiristas* are, in fact, often mingy with praise for colleagues. I once asked Mestre Bamba, one of my teachers in Salvador, what he thought of Mestre Railson, whom I had visited in southern Bahia and who had struck me as exceptionally formidable. *"Uma boa pessoa,"* Bamba replied dismissively, "A good person." I kept private my hunch that Railson could feast upon Bamba for *café da manhã* ("breakfast").

Such parsimony is due in part to the quasi-tribal lineages still running through capoeira. When a *mestre* switches camps, as sometimes happens, it is spoken of in the hushed, conspiratorial tones reserved for death-bed conversions. By and large, though, students remain fiercely loyal to their *mestres* and the style they espouse. So that despite the spread of academies to the rest of Brazil in the 1950s, and later outside the country, Salvador retains its special status as the city of cartwheeling forefathers, the Mecca to which most *capoeiristas* turn in ancestral acknowledgment and pilgrimage. Mestre João Grande, for instance, holds an annual memorial service and *roda* in New York for his own *mestre,* Pastinha; it is strange and marvelous to see a *baiano* born in 1889— just one year after the abolition of slavery in Brazil—connected, by a single living generation, to e-mail era Manhattan.

Capoeira first emigrated to the U.S. in 1975, when Mestre Jelon Vieira, then affiliated with Grupo Senzala (which promulgates an especially high-octane version of *regional*), set up shop in New York. Last summer, Jelon hosted a *roda* in a New York church to celebrate twenty years of capoeira in this country. The event took measure of the substantial growth of capoeira's popularity here—there are now dozens of academies stateside—but also underscored the fact (a welcome one to me) that it has thus far eluded the mainstream.

Unfortunately, at least one member of the general public did not go home a capoeira convert that evening. Mestres Lazaro, of Grupo Palmares, and Bom Jesus, of the notoriously belligerent Capoeira Abadá, had been pushing each other's buttons all night. When neither could trump the other by more sophisticated means, they resorted to pugilism and grappling, finally ending up, in a rum reversal of Calvary, plummeting entwined onto a woman sitting in the front row. Manifestly dismayed at having 400 lbs. of perspiring Brazilian manhood crash-land in her lap, she began bawling. Jelon stopped the proceedings and fulminated to the assembled *capoeiristas,* in both English and Portuguese, that *he* was the master of the *roda* and would eject anyone who insisted on tussling. He is a big, rugged man, hard as titanium nails and with flashing eyes that could freeze Medusa in her tracks; Lazaro and Bom Jesus, whether sulking or out of sheepishness, didn't so much as murmur. When the *roda* resumed, Mestres Ombrinho (my own teacher) and Efraim came out and played a game of flawless craft, precision, and amity; with a little bilingual barking, order had been coaxed back into the circle.

Ombrinho, né Michael Goldstein, began studying in 1979 in San Francisco with Mestre Acordeon, and then under Jelon in

New York. In 1987, he went to Salvador for a year, where he gradually grew disenchanted with the severe Senzala style and fell under the influence of Mestre Nô, the founder of Grupo Palmares, who, Ombrinho felt, best embodied the living capoeira tradition. Although Nô identifies himself as an *Angoleiro,* in practice the Palmares game he has fostered displays traces of both *Angola* and *regional:* played most often at a medium tempo, it oscillates constantly between floorwork and high kicks. Yet it is also less prescriptive than either strict *Angola* or *regional,* and allows each player to search out and tinker with his own idiosyncratic manner.

Despite being in his fifties and having knee problems, Nô is still wiry, nimble as a cat, and able to exhaust several younger players in a row. With his bushy white beard, he looks not unlike a buff, Brazilian version of R. Crumb's Mr. Natural. Perhaps his most striking feature, though, is a pair of eyes mingling confidence, mirth, and an omnidirectional vigilance. It seems inconceivable that he could be duped or taken by surprise, and in this he exemplifies one of capoeira's cardinal maxims: thou shalt always be watchful, even when upside-down and twisted into a human pretzel. But never does Nô's alertness stiffen his game or register as caution. To the contrary, he seems unflappably relaxed, offhand, and even a tad careless—until you try to land a blow on him, at which point he promptly melts away.

Nô's ruse is to appear *aberto* ("open"), tempting his opponent with the bait of vulnerability, while actually remaining *fechado* ("closed"), which in capoeira terms means keeping one's head and torso protected. In fact, *aberto* and *fechado* are, as I discovered, favorite *baiano* antonyms. *Baianos* like to describe themselves as *aberto,* contrasting their expansive, sunny nature to the more reserved, *fechado* one of the *mineiros* (residents of the state of Minas Gerais). Where New Yorkers don their don't-fuck-with-me suits for daily urban war, *baianos* frequently come off, on the surface, as accessible to the point of nudity. And yet they keep their antennae discreetly up, alive to the slightest hint of guile. Aware that things are often not what they seem, *baianos* relish the ambiguity. They even have a hand signal for *ladrão* ("thief"): when someone grinds his thumb into his downturned palm, it means, in essence, "Beware the guy to your left, who is *not* your friend."

As elsewhere, Bahia indulges a degree of romance for its criminal underworld. That *demi-monde* often seemed to me less distinguishable and more eruptive than its U.S. counterpart. For example, I was astonished to learn from my roommates in Salvador that a mutual acquaintance of ours, a garrulous sort who had, as it happens, introduced me to them, had also recently killed a cop in a scuffle. They found nothing remarkable about this: the *PM (polícia militar)* are widely considered the brazenest thugs of all, and are always getting themselves whacked under sordid circumstances.

The local imagination is gripped, in particular, by the figure of the *malandro* ("scoundrel, rascal, thief, swindler, crook," enthuses my dictionary). *Baianos* have a respect, and more than a grudging one, for hoodlum wiliness, which spills over into capoeira in both song—a popular *corrido* celebrates the outlaw Lampeão, whose pickled head was long kept at Salvador's medical school as proof of his demise—and practice: *malandragem* and *malícia* are two of the virtues that *mestres,* Nô and Ombrinho included, most fervently impress upon their students. The former means something like "roguery," the latter usually the same as its English cognate. In capoeira, however, the words take on different, and quite positive, inflections. They refer to a laudable sneakiness of play, the ability to outfox by masking one's true intentions. The capoeira ideal is not to clobber your opponent in an act of naked, lunging aggression, but to so roundly flummox him that he—hapless oaf that he is—blunders into your foot, which you just happen to be ventilating in his airspace.

Malandragem and *malícia* take as many forms as there are *capoeiristas* to practice them. These qualities may manifest as elaborate feints, red herrings dangled before the overeager novice, such as the previously mentioned *aberto/fechado* gambit. *"Buraco velho tem cobra dentro,"* advises a *corrido* ("The old hole has a snake in it"). An archetypal capoeira anecdote tells of a grizzled, creaky *mestre* playing a muscle-bound youngblood. The kid circles the *mestre,* using all his newfangled, bell-and-whistle *floreios.* Then with a single, judiciously placed kick, the *mestre* sends the stunned brat flying from the *roda.* The gaffers smile and nod among themselves at this Odyssean triumph of patient slyness over impetuous brawn.

Other typical tactics include jabbing forked fingers toward an opponent's eyes if you catch him spacing out, pulling a handshake into a head-butt at the beginning or end of a game, and faking injury. Nô likes to play wearing a baseball cap, and will suddenly fling it in your face to momentarily blind or distract you. Many *capoeiristas* are scenery-munching thespians, and can addle with their demeanors alone. Lazaro, for instance, has the rather unsettling habit of chuckling when he plays—an effective psychological maneuver, since it's hard to get mad at someone who seems to be treating the whole thing as a joke, even as he's wiping the floor with you. A few of the nastiest duels I've seen were carried out by contestants with Cheshire-cat grins plastered on their faces.

When I visited Nô at his home one day, he proudly informed me that his dog was a master of *malícia:* it would cozy up to me so long as I stayed in the house, he warned, but then turn upon me the moment I crossed the threshold. Sure enough, the dog soon wallowed affectionately at my feet, a squishy, benevolent, spanielish thing. When it came time to leave, though, I either forgot the second part of Nô's prediction or didn't take it seriously. After stepping out the door, I reached back to pet the nice bow-wow good-bye, only to have it snarl savagely and try to amputate my fingers. Nô was delighted. He said his duplicitous pet had taught me a valuable lesson about being too trusting.

A term that I've never actually heard Brazilians apply to capoeira—although they apply it to practically everything else—is *jeito,* rendered by my dictionary as "aptitude, dexterity, adroitness, skill, knack," but which in fact is one of those untranslatable words that are the glory of any language. As it's used in everyday life, *jeito* expresses the impossible made possible, the seemingly insuperable difficulty solved; I assume Italians have a similar word. Perplexed at how my Brazilian friends could survive on their paltry earnings (Brazil no longer being a cheap country), I would ask them. *"Dar um jeitinho"* was the predictable, maddeningly vague response, *"Give* a little twist to things." I've come to think of capoeira, too, as a silky tissue of *jeitinhos,* of entrapments and Houdiniesque escapes from them. One hallmark of a crackerjack player is his ability to evade the tightest dragnet with effortless panache, finding loopholes in gravity's Napoleonic code; a similar limberness helps him ride out Brazil's economic roller coaster.

The longer I stayed in Bahia, the more I recognized capoeira's inseparability from that teeming place. Previously, I had sniffed at the *mestres'* analogies between capoeira and "life" as so much misty rumination, yet after six months in Salvador I began to see just how closely the *roda* must mirror, for them, everything outside it. The fortitudes demanded by capoeira are, to a considerable extent, those needed on the street: radar, malleability, and calm in situations of capricious uncertainty. This last, in particular, seems to me a key aptitude. *Baianos* are exceptionally hard to raze or bend out of shape, and capoeira depends upon their flexible willingness to accommodate. Not nearly so jealous as Americans of personal space (I never quite got used to people jabbering right in my face), they are comfortable with adapting, at close range, to another player's contortions, and with the shifting, submerged violence that gives capoeira its edge.

69

If a hint of danger adds spice to capoeira, it permeates Brazil far less than I had braced myself for. Despite the country's justifiable reputation for criminality, I find many U.S. cities vastly more menacing. Nearly absent, in Brazil, is the baleful, misanthropic surliness I felt so keenly upon returning to New York. Things can get very hot very fast, true, but in the interim the mood stays jovial and pacific. The one time I did manage to get myself mugged in Salvador—foolishly, I was roaming alleys late at night—the *ladrões* waited patiently while I fished my apartment key from my wallet, then tossed it back to me after taking the money. And after the hardest fall I took while playing capoeira there, when Garrafada swept my standing leg out from under me, he immediately grabbed my hand and pulled me up into a bear hug. In both situations, I had left a flank exposed, and my assailants swiftly capitalized on the mistake—but with a minimum of aggression. While I realize that the former could have gone tragically otherwise, the fact that it didn't made me ponder the dubious likelihood of such a halcyon mugging in New York.

For all its provident focus on street smarts, capoeira partakes equally of the lighter characteristics that have made Brazil globally synonymous with fun. To begin, there is the love of affectionate teasing, evidenced in capoeira as a gadflyish yet comradely pestering of one's fellow player. *Mestres* have the additional perk of saddling you with a derisive nickname, or *apelido.* (Brazilians, as a whole, adore *apelidos:* newspapers commonly identify criminals by both their legal and *favela* monikers, and the nation's deified soccer stars are known as Socrates, Zico, and, of course, Pelé.) At his first *batizado, a* player is given his *apelido,* which typically alludes to, or mocks, some salient quality. Often, the Brazilian fondness for nicknames combines with that for diminutives: Ombrinho means "Little Shoulders," for instance, and the *nome da guerra* of Mãozinha, a Salvador *capoeirista,* is derived, rather cruelly, from the fact of his withered hand. Sabão ("Soap") is known for being slippery, Sabugo ("Corn Cob") is rangy and has flaxen hair, while Cabelo ("Hair") simply has a lot of it. Garrafada means something like "whomped upside the head with a bottle," in reference to an attack he suffered. As for Manga ("Mango") and Pipoca ("Popcorn"), I can only guess; about Come Gato ("Cat Eater") I, being a fanatical aileurophile, don't even want to know.

The peerless Brazilian capacity for gracefully raucous exultation, most vividly proved during Carnival, bursts through everyday in the *roda*. Although there is no shortage of dull, maladroit capoeira (plenty of it perpetrated by yours truly), at its best, capoeira means an effusion of *alegria,* that word of the Romance languages for which "happiness" is a too serene translation; "joy" comes closer to the mark, but still misses the sparkling levity conveyed in the Portuguese. An all-out game produces in its players a kind of endorphic rapture, an absolute fulfillment of the body, that can seem like a minor epiphany, and from which they often emerge beaming and embracing each other. It is, perhaps, a more Dionysian form of the hypnotized euphoria felt by Sufi dervishes and dancers of the tarantella.

And it is here that capoeira most nearly resembles a musical rite, for a player draws his genius from the driving percussion and song enveloping him. Ombrinho frequently chides that lackluster tunes can sap a *roda'*s moxie, whereas, conversely, robust music makes for energetic games. The choice of *toque* establishes the type of play: *Angola* and *São Bento Pequeno* dictate slower games, *São Bento Grande* faster ones, and *Iuna* an acrobatic game open only to *mestres* and advanced students. Within a given *toque,* the three *berimbaus* will conduct learned dialogues of syncopation, while, in the *corridos,* the soloist swaps lyrics back and forth with the rest of the *bateria.*

Seasoned *capoeiristas* even claim a correspondence between song and action. The line *"A pomba voou, o gavião pegou"* ("The pigeon flew, but the hawk took it"), for example, might refer to a player who's just been mauled. *Mestres* are supposedly always sending you encrypted messages and advice through their selection of *corridos*; I, for one, have yet to decipher them. Then there are insult songs, such as the one in which the soloist calls the other players street urchins—*"É tu que é moleque"*—whereupon they shoot back that he, in fact, is the true ragamuffin: *"Moleque é tu."* Sharpest of all, to me, are those *corridos* shot through with memories of slavery:

> Vamos trabalhar
> Vamos plan tar dendê
> Na roda de capoeira
> Nêgo joga para valer.

("Let's go to work, / Let's plant *dendê* [a type of palm]. / In the capoeira circle, / The Negro plays to prove his worth.")

The other instruments in capoeira are subservient, and almost incidental, to the much-celebrated *berimbau,* whose image some players have tattooed on their torsos. *"Esse gunga é o meu, eu não dou a ninguem"* barks one *corrido:* "This *gunga* is mine, I don't give it to anyone" *("gunga"* standing in relation to *"berimbau"* as "hog" does to "motorcycle"). Consisting of a curved hardwood pole, a hollowed-out gourd, a wire pillaged from a discarded automobile tire, a rattle, a stone or coin, and a chopstick-like wand for striking the improbable-looking contraption, the *berimbau* actually descends from an archaic family of instruments known as musical bows.

Like other apparently humble instruments, the *berimbau* can, in the hands of a musician like the renowned Brazilian percussionist Naná Vasconcelos, deliver a surprising complexity of rhythm and tone. To the *capoeirista,* its twangy, plonking sounds beckon him irresistibly into the *roda,* a sensation commemorated in a popular *corrido: "O senhor está me chamando ... para jogar"* ("The man is calling me ... to play"). *Chamar* ("to call") is an important verb in capoeira, the notion being that the *berimbau* player's wandering, unmistakable note summons *capoeiristas* from afar as surely as a Good Humor truck attracts kids from blocks around. Mysteriously, the damn thing has sunk a permanent hook into me; so lodged have its *toques* become, and so closely do I link them to the intense physical pleasure of capoeira, that to hear a *berimbau* calling, yet be unable to respond, would constitute a torture of Medieval magnitude.

Capoeira music falls somewhere between being mere accompaniment and a viable practice in its own right. Recordings proliferate, and the sound has been avidly absorbed into the wider Brazilian idiom, especially by eclectic *baiano* musicians like Caetano Veloso and Gilberto Gil; I once heard an excellent live rendition of a standard *corrido* by Gil and Gal Costa, two of Brazil's top performers. Meanwhile, the *berimbau* has come to stand not only for capoeira, but for Bahia itself, in the way that shamrocks conjure up Ireland and lobsters represent Maine. Salvador now has telephone booths in the shape of *berimbaus,* and the Jewish-*baiana* director Monique Gardenberg cleverly refers to herself as a *"berimbaum."*

Most of all, however, the music serves to remind us that capoeira is an *art*—and I don't mean in the diminished sense implied by "martial art." For its criteria are, at bottom, primarily aesthetic. The highest compliment one *capoeirista* can pay to another is to say that he has *"um jôgo bonito"* ("a beautiful game"). This is the same honorific applied to the supple Brazilian soccer game, which fans bolster and spur on by beating samba drums in the stands; both soccer and capoeira profit from the national intuition, outpatering Pater, that sports, too, should pursue a musical sublimity.

As a writer, I can't help but detect parallels between capoeira and literature. Each game, like each poem, fiction, or essay, involves a thousand half-conscious decisions of lexicon and syntax, tallying up (one hopes) to the capoeira correlative to a signature "voice." The strongest players are original and singular. Some acquire a baroque style sumptuously prinked with *floreios,* the ten-dollar adjectives of Capoeirese; *regional* is especially keen on *floreios* of prodigious technical difficulty. Others prefer a more conversational type of capoeira—granted license, I might even say a witty one. The quicksilver dialogue that goes on between two players can be, in its way, as articulate, nuanced, and deftly amusing as the poshest Elizabethan banter; every sally elicits an immediate, spirited riposte.

It pleases me to speculate that Ovid would have grasped capoeira, with its ceaseless metamorphoses, instantly. Ditto M.C. Escher, whose "Encounter," where two gnomish figures meet and meld with perfect, interlocking economy, bears an uncanny resemblance to a *roda.* Both artists would have appreciated, I think, not only the game's mind-bending plasticity, but its distinct zoomorphism. Much time is spent on all fours, and many capoeira movements boast bestial names, such as the back-flip called *macaco* ("monkey") and a potent, heel-first kick known as a *rabo de arraia* ("tail of the sting ray"). I once saw Railson, face-down, suddenly plant his hands on the floor, bring both his feet over the back of his head, and zap his opponent exactly like a scorpion. The imitation brought the house down (try *that* one at home, boys and girls). Top *capoeiristas* possess the "quick animal certainty" Randall Jarrell admired in Auden; they have a delicious sense of opportunity, and will pounce at a nanosecond's notice.

But despite its feline alacrity—the fastest games leave the observing eye in their dust—capoeira's languor, not its swiftness, is the element I often prize most highly. A lot of the capoeira moments burned into my memory are of little, extraneous touches: Ombrinho marking time by tapping the ground, Anteaus-like, for instance. It is a game of various speeds, and when played slowly can seem a luxurious pantomime. At this mellower rate, the

motions turn exaggerated and sensuous. Not sloppy, though—
the degree of control required for a good slow game is, if anything, greater than for a fast one. A *capoeirista* might begin an *aú*,
freeze it half-way through, playfully punt his opponent as he
comes in for a mock head-butt, collapse inch by inch into a *queda
de rins* ("fall to the kidneys"), his elbow dug into his ribs, then
pivot and slide away.

When well performed, this straightforward sequence alone
can be ravishingly beautiful. Add to it the music plus the *roda's*
sum ambiance, and capoeira becomes, at its finest, a heady event
for the spectator. Many players are immaculately sculpted, a pleasure just to watch, and their gleaming whites stand out against
the lush spectrum of Brazilian skin color. With the bow-shaped
berimbaus, round *pandeiros* ("tambourines")and curvaceous
atabaques ("congas"), the shape of the *roda* itself, and the swirling
circularity of the movements, capoeira has a coherent, and quite
arresting, look; its dominant visual motifs are the crescent, the
parabola, the loop.

In the words of one corrido, *"Não tem lé lé não tem nada"*: basi-
cally, it don't mean a thing if it ain't got that swing. And "that
swing"—the *ginga,* the universal lé lé groove and pulse of dance—
is what brings the game together, along with *axé,* the last untranslatable I'll foist on you, but meaning, in essence, "force" or
"magic." The trick of capoeira is that of any art: making the
aleatory appear inevitable. It accomplishes its hocus-pocus above
all with (to adapt Keats) "the magic foot of chance." The whole
body, though, constitutes both the game's true instrument and
its territory. Across continents, from the days of slavery to those
of manumission, collectively and through its boldest individual
players, capoeira has adventured—profoundly, relentlessly—into
the body's potential for eloquence, for lissom speech.

Notes

Out of distaste for the awkward formulation "he or she," or, worse yet, "s/he," I have chosen—perhaps atavistically—to let the masculine pronoun and possessive suffice throughout. Please read them, however, as indicating both men and women. Once a male preserve, capoeira has recently achieved a degree of sexual equality far beyond most areas of Brazilian (or, for that matter, American) life. I would estimate that nearly half the current students are women, and there is a growing number of female *mestres*. By far the most grueling class I've attended, incidentally, was Mestre Marcia's in San Francisco.

Similarly, I have elected not to litter the page with foot- or endnotes. But I *would* like to acknowledge gratefully the following two books, from which much of the historical background, and other sundry information, is drawn:

Almeida, Bira (Mestre Acordeon), *Capoeira: A Brazilian Art Form.* Berkeley: North Atlantic Books, 1986.

Lewis, J. Lowell, *Ring of Liberation: Deceptive Discourse in Brazilian Capoeira.* Chicago: The University of Chicago Press, 1992.

Master of Applied Cowardice

John F. Gilbey

"After all, th'only ole, reliable,
safe an' sane sport is croquet."

ANONYMOUS

A Harvard player in the 1894 football game with Yale landed a right cross to the immortal jaw of Yale's Frank Hinkey. "My friend," said Hinkey, "if you hit me another like that you'll break your hand."

Hinkey was tough but he wasn't indestructible. What the vignette shows is grand panache,* or to put it more plainly, *style*. You remember how Cyrano spouted poetry in the process of undoing a bad "un." That was panache. This flair isn't restricted to class: I've seen farmers exhibit it as often and as easily as college men.

---

* Corneille was the French writer who put *panache* into the language. In the same way Chinese warrior-nobles had graciously offered 2,000 years earlier, a French officer at Fontenoy says to officers of King George II: "You gentlemen may fire first." That is *panache*.

But one of the best at all three—fighting, poetry, and *panache*—was a college man, a professor named Jed Connor. I met Jed years ago at a poetry congress in Louisville, home of beautiful horses, fast women, and Kentucky bourbon, only one of which I'd sell much of my soul for. I had been told about Jed by Bill Paul, who had taught him his course in "applied cowardice."

Let me explain. The first and last lesson of any worthwhile martial art is the avoidance of fighting. It is not enough simply to espouse this as an ethic. It has to be taught ... and learned. And just as assiduously as the more offensive mechanics.

Bill Paul, former west coast judo champ, actually has created and taught such a course in recent years. In the course Bill teaches a full-range of aspects, such as graceful exits, individuation, appeals to ego, ego salvage, the balance of power, and the possibilities of humor. Then, using the Asian martial arts as a base, Bill teaches the tyro functional nonviolent defense techniques of posture, movement, recovery, disengagement, and escape. (Rumor hath it that Bill perfected these techniques from field experience in peace marches in which Hell's Angels—ever on the wrong side—were wont to assault the passive. But I understand that at that time Bill didn't have a good grasp of the ideas he later developed—and often cheated.)

The course is not easy. Peace is always harder than war. It is rigorous; he tosses his pupils into simulated combat with never a backward glance. In controlled situations, Bill would teach an offensive karate group and a defensive "cowardice" group separately for a semester and then have them compete. The result was always the same—the defensive group won.

Bill told me that Jed, a former golden glove champ and judo 3-dan, was his best student, a guy with moxie, and a good poet to boot. So I wrote and shook hands with Jed by letter, and the first chance I got I went on down to Caintuck. He invited me out to his ramshackle abode where I met his deep-eyed wife, Sarah, and his three kids.

I relished verse and had published some, but he was a real poet. And he had comfortable chairs.

"Poetry," he started, "is the smile on the face of truth. The smile says I will be here or someplace very like here when the mountains are flat.

"Poetry is life just as fighting is life. And just as a good poem is never completed, only abandoned, so fighting is a never-ending process. No one was ever a perfect fighter. 'The unflawed pot,' you know."

While discussing poetry, we were eating homemade donuts (what the cowboys used to call "bear find") and drinking superb coffee. Ah, coffee, it's getting a bad name these days. We can spend $300 billion for defense during détente but we come down hard on the evils of the black stuff. Why? Because it will kill you. Sure, but the things we eat and the air we breathe and the thoughts we think do that just as rapidly.

Voltaire drank fifty cups a day and Balzac, forty. Talleyrand liked it "black as the devil, hot as hell, pure as an angel, and sweet as love."

Now, I don't drink much, a cup or two a day. Jamaican Blue Mountain when I can get it, otherwise Kona, Yunnan, or Colombian will do. I know most people abuse it by over drinking and by swallowing the ersatz instant bilge. It gives you pause to watch some folks sit for twenty minutes over a cup of instant coffee.

Nope. Coffee is getting a bad rap. There comes a time when it is incomparable, a time caught beautifully by J. Frank Dobie: "I want to sit down with some old rawhide and listen to him blow his coffee, listen to him make a kind of solemn—joyful noise unto the Lord, an unconscious characterizing expressive of the mighty response of his whole body to coffee...."

But poetry wasn't the end of Jed. He shared my interest in the martial and my abhorrence of modern war. We might have been different in another time, but World War I ended chivalry. Before

79

that, one had conducted and been part of a relationship with the enemy. Afterwards, technology alienated every soldier from the actions he himself took.

Jed also liked chess and was a pretty fair hand at it, but was smart enough not to take it seriously. "Most great chess players are mad. Did you ever hear of Steinitz?" he asked.

"Sure, wasn't he the one so all-fired deluded that he thought he could move the pieces without touching them?"

"Right, he was a pip. Once challenged God, offering him pawn and move. Question is: does chess drive people like him crackers or is there something about chess that draws wacky people? I don't know."

"I remember Marcel Duchamp writing that chess was important because it had absolutely no social function."

"Keerect. And Chesterton more than once urged doing the meaningless, the thing with no utility in life as a good path. So he'd agree with Duchamp. But I'm not sure that this nonutility had anything to do with making chess masters mad. On the contrary. To do something for its own sake apart from any accruing utility strikes me as something that would drive a man sane, not crazy."

But most of the time we spent on what turned out to be a too short weekend, we talked about his brand of fighting or, more concretely, nonfighting. Bill Paul had demonstrated the system and had touched a sympathetic chord in me. I first gave Jed some of my views on it.

Avoidance should not be construed as cowardice. In this context I am reminded of a delicious story by Bertold Brecht. A town is conquered by vandals and the high priest's home taken over by the commander. He brusquely tells the priest: "You will clean my house, prepare my food, and cater to my every wish. You will be my slave. Do you consent?" Without answering, the priest sets about scrubbing the floor and performing other menial jobs. He serves the commander for ten years, at the end of which the Vandal dies and his army is overthrown. The priest buries him; then spits on the grave and answers, "No."

The art of any real fighting system is in never having to use what you've learned. Thus, it is aimed at you and no one else. The old phrase "judo teaches you to run with confidence" still rings with the profound. I've always—well, almost always—believed and practiced this.

Once years ago in Chicago I went into a small Chinese grocery with a young man who was trying to pump me for "wisdom." As I entered the store, I must have brushed too close to a behemoth in a World War II khaki coat. I was selecting some groceries when the young man approached and from the side of his mouth told me that the big guy had taken offense at me and that I should watch out. As I took my purchases to the front counter, I looked khaki over with peripheral vision. He was 6'1", 220 pounds, aged forty-eight or thereabouts. And pretty well soused.

I didn't look directly at him for the same reason one doesn't look a snarling threatening dog in the eye—the look becomes a challenge. But I kept part of an eye on him and my ears tuned toward him. The little Chinese owner must have noticed because he swiped his cleaver down meaningfully near my groceries. Khaki shuffled out the door.

As I was paying, the young man again came over, saying, "He's waiting outside." In our previous discussion I had tried to make the point that the greatest fighting skill exists in never using that skill. Now I tested the youngster.

"Do you really want to see some sophisticated boxing?" I asked him. He salivated like What's-His-Name's dogs. "I sure would."

"Okay, then watch," I told him. Then turning to the little grocer, "Do you have a back door?"

He did, showed it to us, and we exited without incident. Outside, I could see the boy was disappointed.

"What good," I asked him, "would it do to belabor a poor drunk? All it would do is increase the violence in the world by meeting his alcohol-induced hate with your own. It would certainly not add to one's knowledge of boxing."

He pretended to believe—but I don't think he did. Conditioned by a desperately confused and violent culture, he saw the best solutions as sanguine ones.

We might remember the story of the old jiujutsu master whose dojo was in the midst of a small wood. A little path led to his eighteen-mat dojo. On the narrow path one day, someone had tethered a demented jackass. As the first student going to practice approached the animal, it lashed out with a foot, breaking his leg. He started to crawl home, but then, wondering how the others would fare, he hid in the bushes to watch. Soon another student approached the animal but, being more skillful than the first, he was able to turn slightly and the kick only shattered his kneecap. He, too, jumped in the bushes to monitor developments. The best *jiujutsuka* came along shortly, walked right up to the animal, sensed something, and did a beautiful turn and the kick missed him entirely. Afterwards he hid in the bushes to see how the old master would handle the mad beast. Finally the old man came along the path, decrepit and full of years but withal graceful. As he approached the jackass he paused, walked around the other side of him, and proceeded down the path. His jiujutsu art was avoidance.

Then it was Jed's turn, sitting there in that rumpled suit: "It is a law of nature that if a species' weapons are not dangerous, the inhibitory mechanism is absent. This may be one of the reasons man is so violent: in comparison with most animals, his weapons are extremely ineffectual. Whereas snakes and bears wrestle, central European sand lizards take turns biting each other without breaking the skin, and a wolf beaten in a tussle offers his throat to another, these things inhibit use of lethal weapons. But man's natural weapons are not lethal. There is no code restricting the use of the rudimentary weapons he has.

"A part of nature's inhibitory mechanism is to give the defeated room to escape. If he is caged with the victor, death may ensue. Running room is necessary. If, for example, monkeys, rats, and hamsters are prevented from flight, death is frequent.

"In Bill's system, which I've adapted to my own boxing and judo, we make that running room and use it to its fullest. We become geniuses of the fast get-away. This makes our system the most self-defensive in the catalog. Now, most Asian fighting arts claim that they are self-defensive and never, never aggressive.

"And some truly are. T'ai chi, correctly taught, doesn't even relate function to posture. And there is an Okinawan style of karate, *shuri-no-te*. The *art-of-not-fighting*, which is premised on the sane notion that walking away is better than causing harm to someone who is apparently out of harmony with himself, nature, or his fellow beings. And there are a few judo teachers who teach the art as it was first created by Jigoro Kano: enlightened jacketed wrestling.

"But practice doesn't live up to theory. The result is that too many martial art types can hardly wait for a chance to vent their spleen and knuckles on some poor unoffending fighter. Gichin Funakoshi, the great Okinawan karate expert, really believed in an ethic, however. In fact, his motto was *karate ni sent naski* (karate has no offense). But in his autobiography he acknowledged how quickly many students departed from the ideal.

"Our method is systematic and scientific. And psychologically sound. It is not trickery. You know the assassin bug?" I didn't.

"Well, when it is attacked by an ant, it releases a fluid from its abdomen and offers it to the ant. The ant likes the stuff and munches it so greedily that he fails to notice the bug's forelegs slowly encircling its neck."

"Shades of the *thugee*," I put in.

"Right," said he. "While that kind of trickery may touch a poetic impulse, it is really a cheap shot, oblique rather than direct violence. As devious as it is imaginative, but essentially as violent as violence. Our system isn't like that. It is simply one of educated movement shorn of deceit.

"The three important things are time, distance, and exposure. All are crucial. The attacker will attempt to make his move as rapidly across as short a distance with as little exposure as possible. Your job is to extend all these factors.

"Let's start with the preliminaries, which are as vital here as they are in love. The way you stand and act may actually cause an attack. So try to stand out of an opponent's immediate zone— defined as his height's distance away from him. And stand at a diagonal to him. If you stand frontal, he may regard it as threatening. Your hands obviously should not be clenched or on your hips or even crossed in front of your chest. Any of these he may perceive as threatening. He may even be alarmed by hands held in back of you. So hold them open in full sight.

"Now, the typology of the attacker is that in a crisis (or what he views as one) he takes on tunnel vision; his focus is limited to a narrow strip immediately ahead of him. Work to keep out of this tunnel. Try to avoid sharp angles in your stance. Have as loose and rounded an attitude as possible. Keeping out of his territory with just such an inoffensive posture and mien may be sufficient to preclude the attack. At a minimum, if he is adept in the art of premature self-defense, these precautions may prevent his suckering you.

"But maybe they won't. Then you go into your avoidance routine. If he does a two-hand choke on your throat, simply put the fingers of your left hand against his trachea and push off. This will bounce you away from him backwards.

"Or say he closes the distance, sets himself with his left foot forward and throws a right fist. This time, thrust against his chest with your left hand while kicking off backward. The rebound will let you avoid his fist easily. It is impossible for him to hit you if your thrust is timed right. And the thrust can be against his arm as well as his chest.

"Moving back is done by pushing off your front foot as you push off his body. It can be a chopping, rapid step as you take the front foot toward the rear, push off, and repeat. Or it can be a big floating sequence. It all depends on the attack itself. Accompanying the step, keep slapping out nonoffensively with your hands at his eyes, all the while trying to get him to desist.

"The key, of course, is that you extend time, distance, and exposure by moving back. The thrust is not an attack—simply a means of propelling yourself back. Now as you move back, your hands are kept in a Western boxing position and your feet don't cross.

"So he's missed. You've tried to talk him out of it as you've moved away from him. He probably didn't even notice your thrust. But he knows he's missed. He didn't get you quick and close. And he's been exposed. People who didn't notice the oral dispute now are aware of the physical. He's getting exposure and he feels foolish. So that may end it.

"Or it may not. He makes another approach, you leap back, and he has to take an extra step round the corner to confront you (this because of your diagonal stance). But he catches you and strikes again. Thrust and leap away. You can keep this up all day. But he can't. The factors have run out on him. In fact, Ray Lunny, the Stanford boxing coach, uses pretty much the same tactics and, past fifty, will take on anyone without getting his hair mussed.

"The basic exercises in this method (hell, it's almost methodless; all it requires of the practitioner is extreme cowardice) are thrusting off a wall in such a way that the legs don't cross and are then ready for the next backward move. The rest is simply avoidance and your body can be trained to it by a lot of backward running and various sports. The thing is easy because it's natural. You already have the skill of hand and eye and leg coordination—it comes with a ball glove—all you have to do is adapt it to this system.

"The best preparation for this system is in wrestling and Western boxing. These teach you good footwork and also show you how to be comfortable in close. But they also can give you an attacking tendency which could be fatal. So you've got to be selective in what you take from them.

"Handball is perhaps the best adjunctive sport for any system of combative including this one. It is a fast game, requires rapid eyes, and the use of all body components. The feet are synchronized to brain and eye and must go in all directions, backwards as often as frontwards. The body is forced to play high as often as low. So it covers a whole range of effort. Tennis is much more limited."

The best example in western boxing of carrying this off with élan was Jimmy Wilde who, at 100 pounds, won the flyweight championship of the world and often boxed featherweights (126 pounds). Being so light, he obviously couldn't trade punches with many of the fighters he faced. Instead, he would invariably move to the rear, fending off the volleys as they came, blocking, slipping (taking the head laterally out of the path of incoming punches), ducking, and then countering. And, oh, he could counter! His knockout record was 56%, an astounding percentage against men who were so much bigger.

"But in the ring Wilde was much more constrained than a person in the street need be. We can run and try to hide. He couldn't."

" 'Bicycle' Bob Pastor tried to against Louis," I put in. "He ran like a thief and survived the first ten rounds of the first fight, and the only way he got a rematch was to agree to a twenty round bout. Before that one, Louis said 'He can run, but he can't hide.' He was right. He got Pastor in the eleventh round of the second go. Jeffries and Langford also had trouble with runners. Trying to catch one guy, Langford knocked him out—believe it or not!—by hitting him in the buttocks! Another guy, Jeffries knocked down with a right to the coccyx."

"Right. They had trouble, but they were still able to get their man because of the restricting ring. But we don't have that problem. Space is our ally and our antagonist's enemy.

"That's why I've found that one of the most necessary and effective ingredients of this method is running backward for two miles each day. This is hard, tedious, and boring work, but it is absolutely essential. My better boys I even have do wind sprints backwards, and there is one—Steve Kelley—who can do a 100 yards in under seventeen seconds."

"Not as good as Bill 'Bojangles' record," I said, "but he's gaining."

"If you can outrun your oncoming opponent then there is often no need to close with him. And, attacking takes more out of a man than defending. To the long distance and sprint ability going backward, I add the lateral move going either way. This gives us four avenues if you count going into the man which we will do but only in a pinch. He can follow us down these dark mean streets but always, because he is reacting, he will be a shade behind. If he catches up, we permutate him with shoves, slaps, and if necessary, actual punches. Even here we first attempt evasion, but if strikes or throws are required we use them—but only for temporary effect. The stress is always on movement."

I interrupted him here to praise the system. Most so-called new systems I had found came from men unable to stand the discipline of an orthodox method. The result was that most were as inefficient as a trombone player with TB.

But then I made a mild rebuttal of the system, saying, "You don't have to understand Werner Heisenberg's Theory of Indeterminacy to know that human knowledge is incomplete. Nothing is known for sure. Heisenberg concluded that it is tough enough to measure one aspect of a sitting duck precisely, but when motion is introduced, all bets are off. What the esteemed scientist didn't realize is that the indeterminacy or uncertainty of measurement applies even without the motion.

"It is commonly believed that a fighter must move; otherwise he is vulnerable to an attacker. It ain't necessarily so. Some Tibetan and Chinese master boxers stand very still and wait for the opponent's move, believing that *any* move the opponent makes provides an opening for a riposte. They use no fancy footwork, and they hold their arms still. To them, most foot and arm maneuvers are more a function of a boxer's nervousness than of a strategy. Movement does several things, all bad: (1) it betrays nervousness, (2) it shows a posture that the attacker can utilize, and (3) it blocks the meridians, impedes blood and energy, and hampers breathing. In short, for the body to respond efficiently it cannot be a divided force. The energy that fells the attacker is whole-body energy, delivered in a flash.

"These masters must have sensed something else. Psychologist John Hughlings has recently noted that the human eye and its cerebral anchor can stay focused on a static object for only a minute or so. After which some sort of adjustment is necessary. You blink—and even though this is done in one fortieth of a second, it's a big opening for some boxers—close your eyes, shake your head, etc., and then restart."

Jed shook his shaggy head. "I grant your thesis and proofs. But, John, your master boxer is not going to assault anyone. He's not the one this system has to deal with. We are dealing with hung-up crazies who want to pile on us like Ossa on Pelion. It all reduces to the pivotal proposition: if God had wanted us to fight, why did he give us legs?"

The man who thinks he knows it all is a pain in the neck to those of us who really do. But Jed's rebound was resoundingly on the mark. It was true and made the system all the more pleasing.

"Your method then is so geared to rapid retreat, it wouldn't know how to be offensive?" I asked.

"Not quite," he answered. "You've heard of the Parthian Shot? Well, it got its name from the Parthians, a group of Persians who emigrated from Scythia to what is now Iran in the first century BC. These Parthians were notorious for their method of warfare in which they would fake a pell-mell retreat when the first spear was hurled at them. Shortly thereafter though, they would wheel around and catch the over-anxiously pursuing enemy unawares with a quick, massive volley. That last and most effective shot is the Parthian Shot. And we're not above using it. It doesn't have to be a thing of beauty or a joy forever. Perfection can be death in the street. You don't need a clean throw or strike. All you need is a bump or half-trip; anything to make him stumble will suffice to let you extricate or, if you must, get yours in. But I stress we use it only in an emergency. Most of the time, we just run. *That* is our art."

Intermission

External
and Internal

Ron Sieh

EXTERNAL AND INTERNAL

There are two traditions of Chinese martial arts and they are the so-called **external** (or outer) and **internal** schools or **Wai Chia** and **Nei Chia**. These two schools are also called **Shaolin** and **Wu Dang**. It is said that the *external* martial arts, which Shaolin is said to be, are mainly concerned with *strengthening the muscles and bones and achieving the proper execution of technique,* while *internal* arts are more concerned with the *cultivation of Chin (intrinsic power) and the more "energetic" skills of listening to and reading an opponents movement and presence.*

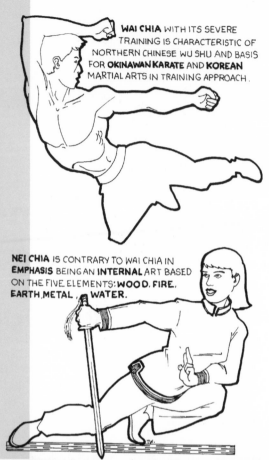

WAI CHIA WITH ITS SEVERE TRAINING IS CHARACTERISTIC OF NORTHERN CHINESE WU SHU AND BASIS FOR **OKINAWAN KARATE** AND **KOREAN** MARTIAL ARTS IN TRAINING APPROACH.

NEI CHIA IS CONTRARY TO WAI CHIA IN **EMPHASIS** BEING AN **INTERNAL** ART BASED ON THE FIVE ELEMENTS: **WOOD, FIRE, EARTH, METAL, WATER.**

THE EXTERNAL IS HARD, OFTEN CALLED A HARD STYLE. KARATE IS OFTEN CONSIDERED A "HARD" STYLE, HARDER AND FASTER BEING TWO OFTEN USED WORDS BY INSTRUCTORS TO STUDENTS.

THE INTERNAL IS SOFT AND RELAXED, MORE CIRCULAR, TIMING BEING MORE IMPORTANT THAN SPEED, WHILE BODY MECHANICS AND OPENNESS TO THE OPPONENTS INTENT ARE MORE IMPORTANT THAN THE EXECUTION OF A SPECIFIC TECHNIQUE.

For example when faced with a punch from a right hand coming toward your face an external or hard stylist would see this as a challenge and a problem to be thwarted and overcome, usually by **blocking** the punch and trying to **hit** or **kick** the puncher. An internal martial artist could avoid

the punch through **listening** and **dodge** the punch **without interfering with it**, perhaps even use the puncher's own force to "help" him off balance and throw him. In Aikido, a Japanese internal art, the attacker would (ideally), not be harmed. This was important to Ueshiba the founder (if not some of his followers). There would be a quality of openness to the event that the hard stylist would not have.

ASIDE FROM HARD BLOCK **EXTERNALS** AND CIRCULAR EVASIVE **INTERNAL** STYLES ARE THE EXHIBITIONIST HARD STYLE OF ICE BLOCK SHATTERING AND CHI FORCE REPELLING OF AN OPPONENT.

CRUMP!

Instead of trying to interfere with the punch and direct the event to their advantage through force, the event would be seen, listened to, adhered to, blended with, and concluded. An internal martial artist feels the situation and fills the holes. Or not.

Actually, there are not any entirely internal or external martial arts (Shaolin and Wu Dang more accurately describe the categories), but there are internal or external martial artists. The hard styles of Shaolin or Karate can be done as delicately and naturally as a soft or internal style.

That is when the internal "style" is demonstrated by internal artists. I've seen a lot of Aikido and T'ai Chi Ch'uan which are considered internal styles done in a contrived and stubborn style. External to internal is a natural progression of skill rather than any particular art. My Tae Kwon Do teacher (Tae Kwon Do is a Korean art) was, when I studied with him, an internal martial artist while his art, Tae Kwon Do, is typically considered hard and external.

Any situation or relationship—including one of potential violence—demands a certain openness, a "feel" for the lover's or enemy's or friend's intentions. To "feel" an opponent's intention requires feeling our own vulnerability—and that is an asset rather than something to deny. Denial is denial: to rather not feel something in ourselves is to deny the situation as it is, to misread it.

Misreading is the number one reason people "lose" fights, or miss the Frisbee, lose at Chess, miss the ball, trip, injure themselves, get in fights, etc. etc.

Something that all Chinese martial arts have in common is the notion of cultivation and storing energy in the Tan Tien (in Chinese) or Hara (Japanese). This is a point in the human body two or three fingers' width below the navel and perhaps one-half to one and one-half inches inside the abdomen, depending on the tradition ... or, more importantly, where the person *feels* it is. It is where the breath is concentrated in many Chi Kungs and where one's vitality is stored. Chi or energy

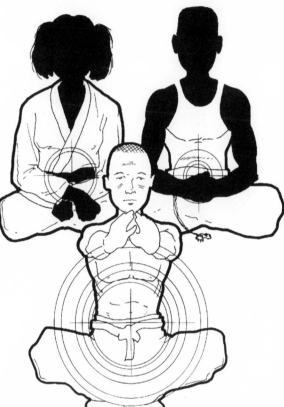

is also central to Chinese martial arts. In fact, it is central to all martial arts, though, more often than not, it is spoken of more or less after the basic techniques of the art are learned. The internal branch of martial arts is called Wu Dang after a range of mountains in Hubei province. T'ai Chi Ch'uan (T'ai Chi Ch'uan means Supreme Ultimate Absolute, Ch'uan is boxing), the most popular of Wu Dang arts, was created by Chang Seng Feng according to the legend ascribed to by the Yang family. Chang Seng Feng, apparently already skilled in Shaolin (and a Taoist), retreated to the Wu Dang mountains in 1327 and there witnessed a battle between a snake and a crane.

(In fact the witnessing of animals fighting is found in the origin stories of several martial arts.) Anyway, Chang Seng Feng was impressed with how the snake did not fight the strength of the crane or did it block the crane's blows -- it avoided them. Chang Seng Feng thereupon realized the advantages of yielding to force rather than fighting it, which is a central theme in T'ai Chi Ch'uan. Chang Seng Feng's birthday is said to be on April 9th and is celebrated by T'ai Chi players worldwide.

> **THE INTERNAL ARTS ARE CONSIDERED TO BE A BLEND OF TAOIST ENERGETICS AND BREATHWORK, AS WELL AS THE TAOIST APPROACH TO THE WORLD AND MARTIAL TECHNIQUE.**

Philosophically, one cannot speak of Chinese internal martial arts without speaking of Taoism. The Tao (pronounced "Dow"), is the equivalent of the Dharma in Buddhism, God in Judaism and Christianity, or "What Is" or "Suchness" in Zen.

Lao Tzu

The most famous and well read work on Taoism is the "Tao Te Ching" or "The Way and the Power." According to legend, it was written by Lao Tzu around 500 BC (Lao Tzu means old teacher), but no one really knows if he wrote it or if the "Tao Te Ching" was written by several authors over a period of time. The legend says that Lao Tzu, being fed up with the folly of his fellow humans and their chasing after worldly gain, decided to give it up and head for the hills.

At the city gate he found the guard would not let him do so unless he **wrote down** his wisdom, thus the "Tao Te Ching."

Lao Tzu, unlike Confucius, disdained social convention and also ... religion. **The experience of Tao does not come from faith or acting the way we think we should, but from the depth of our own nature.** There is a quality in Lao Tzu's Taoism of "beginner's mind," of raw, naked experience, unencumbered by philosophy or rules. Chapter 18 is one of my favorites:

> WHEN THE GREAT TAO IS FORGOTTEN, PHILANTHROPY AND MORALITY APPEAR.
> INTELLIGENT STRATEGIES ARE PRODUCED, AND GREAT HYPOCRISIES EMERGE.
> WHEN THE FAMILY HAS NO HARMONY, PIETY AND DEVOTION APPEAR.
> THE NATION IS CONFUSED BY CHAOS, AND LOYAL PATRIOTS EMERGE.

Taoist martial artists or internal martial artists approach the experience of combat with this quality of spontaneity and lack of contrivance.

There are different approaches to Taoism. Confucius was really into virtue, familial piety and

one's place in the structure of society. I like to say that Confucius would have one obey and faithfully fulfill one's societal and familial obligations to realize Tao, and the Lao Tzu "approach" is to naturally realize the Tao through deep yet

simple opening to the Tao. One is a process of duty and addition, the other a process of openness and subtraction—subtracting the layers of socialization, contrived duty, and obligation. You can see which of the two the Chinese government ascribes to, and which, in turn, can be used to justify a

bureaucratic government. The other approach—the openness and spontaneity of Lao Tzu and Chuan Tzu Taoism—is called Wu Wei.

Wu Wei, or "non-action," is not doing nothing, but doing nothing in excess.

Excess can mean eating when you are not hungry, sleeping when you are not tired, defending yourself when you don't have to, being afraid of something that doesn't exist, blocking a punch that isn't there, wanting to be different than you are, thinking too much, being tense, worrying, making excessively long sentences and the list goes on.

REALIZING ONE'S OWN NATURE IS THE HEART OF TAO.

INTERNAL ARTS

The arts described so far are all considered Wai Dan or external school. Nei Dan or Nei Chia, which means internal school, are the arts originating from Chan Sang Feng. Wu Dang is where Chang Sang Feng created his T'ai Chi Ch'uan, the external are Shaolin. The internal arts are T'ai Chi Ch'uan, Hsing I Ch'uan, and Pakua Chang and have been influenced by Taoist thought, Chi Kung, and healing work and are generally done in a more relaxed (but not excessively relaxed) manner.

THIS IS A PICTURE ABOUT TWO KUNG FU MASTERS: MONKEY KUNG FU MASTER PAULIE ZINK, (ALSO AN ADEPT IN TAOIST YOGA: CHI KUNG), AND TAI CHI CHUAN MASTER DOC FAI WONG WHO (ALONG WITH HAWKINS CHEUNG AND MARSHALL HO) IS ONE OF THE FOREMOST EXPONENTS OF TAI

CHI CHUANS **HEALING** AND **DESTRUCTIVE QUALITIES**.
The End.

WHY DON'T YOU GET OFF YOUR REAR AND HELP ME CLEAN UP?!

MARTHA YOU ARE TROUBLED ABOUT MANY THINGS. THE BEAUTY OF LAO TZU IS HOW IT FREES ME FROM SO MANY CUMBERSOME CONVENTIONS.

THE BUSY CONFUCIUST AND THE LAO TZUIST

Part II

Are Women
the Weaker Sex?

Rene Denfeld

The first time I got into the ring to spar, I was so nervous, my knees were shaking. Jess fitted the damp, smelly leather helmet neatly over my head and ears, leaving my face exposed. He laced the fourteen-ounce training gloves on next. They felt like foreign growths on my hands, heavy and bulky, and I flexed my fingers inside their sweaty interiors, feeling the empty spaces.

With the gloves on, I was helpless as a baby. I couldn't blow my nose, wipe the sweat out of my eyes, or do anything else requiring fingers. Jess popped my mouthpiece in with quick fingers that tasted, briefly, of salt.

I set my face into composed lines, shuffled my feet, and tried not to let anyone know just how scared I really was. The men gathered around. They watched, mouths ajar at the novelty of a woman entering the ring, until the coaches began bellowing, "Get back to work."

The eighteen-year-old Hispanic man who had been picked as my sparring partner—because of his weight of 118 pounds—was already in the ring, shadowboxing to loosen up. The bright lights of the gym glinted off his muscled arms and narrow shoulders. He was dressed in high-top orange shoes, a light tank top, and soft cotton trunks. The heavy leather belt (for crotch protection) fitted snugly over his trunks, cupping his groin. Under the shadow of his helmet, his face—with heavy lips and brown eyes—looked blank in concentration. I learned later that his name was Octavio.

There was only one thought in my mind: I am going to get hit.

The idea frightened me more than I had imagined. Once I realized—at gut level—that getting punched was unavoidable, I ran into twenty-six years of social indoctrination like a brick wall. I was afraid I would freeze. I was afraid it would hurt. I had visions of women being hit in the movies: cringing, helpless, pleading.

Jess gave me a careful, considering look. Then he pointed his head toward the ring.

I climbed through the ropes and stood on the gritty, unfamiliar canvas. I raised my fists. The gloves, padded, loomed like red balloons in front of me. For a second, I couldn't remember if I had my fists turned properly. I couldn't remember anything. My mind 'went blank'; my few months of training vanished. I took a deep breath. Okay, here goes, I thought.

The bell rang. My sparring partner looked up at me from under his helmet, bit his lips, and crossed himself. He shifted forward slightly, his legs moving under the long trunks. I forced myself forward, uncertain, my feet numb and clumsy.

My training returned: I threw out a few jabs.

Nervous, he responded: a stinging jab to my nose. I lunged at him, overexcited, trying to hit him with my jab, throwing wild rights. He slapped me politely on the ribs, landed a few more jabs.

And I thought, that doesn't hurt so bad.

Somehow, that realization was more exciting and fulfilling then I could ever have imagined. I was being hit by a man. But I wasn't falling to pieces. I was going to be okay.

I hit him back as well as I could, lacking his skill yet having just as much perseverance. Bobbing and weaving across the ring, breathing raspily through our mouthpieces, we flicked jabs, rights, and body blows. I was going too fast, getting too wound up. Jess made a soothing sound from the side of the ring.

We kept eye contact the entire time. Even in the heat of battle—how curious, that tempestuous term for what turns out to be so quiet, almost peaceful—I noticed little things: his eyelashes, the shadow by the cusp of his nose. A bubble of mucus appeared under his left nostril. We were both prickly with heat, and breathing raggedly. Our faces were scant inches apart, close enough to kiss.

Thwack. I saw that coming, the right, and still walked directly into it. When you get smacked in the nose like that, it is quick, stunning—painless in an odd way, and yet disturbing: a thick, diffuse, blotting sensation. Desperate, I plowed into him, and he captured my arms in a quick clinch, turned me deftly against the ropes, and spun me out again. Jess made a snorting, derisive noise from the side of the ring. I barely had time to feel like a fool (I learned how to store these moments for later self-castigation) before we were hitting each other again.

Time held still, counted only by blows: a jaw-rattling left hook to my chin, a surprisingly stunning straight right, a jabbing left peppering my face. Later, I became aware how much he was babying me—how light the punches actually were. At the time, they seemed more than enough. Boxers call it "glove-shy": the sense of shock at being hit, not because of pain, but more from the invasion of privacy, the body shock of it. You close your eyes and wince involuntarily. Only through sparring do you eventually lose your glove shyness, learn how to look straight into your partner's eyes, and cease to blink when hit.

I became aware of a stitch under my ribs, sweat trickling under my helmet, my nose running. I could hear all the sounds of the gym—Jess giving calm advice from the side of the ring, someone hitting the heavy bag, guys conversing in quiet tones, the ten-seconds-to-go buzzer—yet at the same time it seemed that the world had narrowed down to just us, two bodies pitted against each other. I got through with a strong right hook to his rib cage and felt a rush of hot pleasure to see his eyes blink in startled pain.

When the bell rang, we stopped immediately. We didn't grin at each other and slap our gloves together. That would come later. But we did smile shyly at each other. And I walked out of that ring feeling as if I were floating. I had done it.

My face was tender, and later it bruised slightly. I lay on the couch that evening, seraphic with exhaustion, nearly bursting with pride.

My brother tells me that women shouldn't be allowed to compete physically against men, because men are stronger.

I think of my brother's words and I think about sparring with Octavio, and the countless times I have sparred with men since. Whom else am I going to spar against, without any other women in the gym who compete?

Octavio was more than my first sparring partner. He was a revelation. I had never competed physically with a man before, and certainly not on such intimate—and equal—terms. His arms, his legs, the shape of his torso—they were nearly the same as mine. We had more in common than not, outside of his cup, my chest guard, my wider hips, and his longer legs. He was far more skilled than I, but mostly because he'd been training longer.

At that time, most of the men at the gym were much better than I. They could hold me off with their fists, show off. Questions of superiority were moot. The playing field wasn't equal, and there was no pretense it should be. Beginning fighters always start with more experienced fighters, because putting two green boxers in the ring is just asking for an out-of-control punching match. A more experienced fighter can teach without hurting a newer fighter or getting hurt himself.

Now sometimes I'm the more experienced fighter climbing through the ropes. I discover the feeling that Octavio must have felt with me: how careful experience can make you. Usually the fighter is male, and so the status has been reversed. These newer fighters cannot hide behind chivalry. There have been times when I've gone into the ring with men who were almost incapacitated by the fear they would get beaten and embarrassed by a girl. Each time in the ring can be a struggle.

When I suggest to my brother that maybe some women are just as strong as some men—or that maybe strength difference doesn't matter as much as skill—he responds with derision. Men shouldn't compete against women like that, he says, because it is unfair.

Men, he says, are just stronger.

Maybe men are not stronger—or at least not always, and not in the ways we assume.

I, too, had always thought that by nature men are stronger than women. I assumed that they must have some magical property to their muscles, some innate difference in fiber, structure, or size that makes a bicep that looks just as stringy as mine burst with male virility.

It came as a surprise to learn that this isn't the case. Strength differences between the sexes are not that profound, nor are they set in stone. Generally, women are about two-thirds as strong as men. This is partially due to men's greater size (they have more muscle mass). When researchers compare men and women of the same height and weight, they find differences substantially decline.

Many such differences in strength are based on activity. The same studies that show men are stronger also indicate that this disparity is concentrated in the upper body, less so for the lower body. This is because both sexes use their leg muscles in daily walking and in exercises such as jogging, while men are far more likely to engage in exercises such as weight lifting or to work in

109

jobs that involve digging, carrying, or heavy lifting—activities that target their arms and shoulders.

In January of 1996, the U.S. Army released a study confirming that women are capable of performing all the military tasks once reserved for men, providing they are given the training. The army discovered that women can easily increase upper-body strength to meet the most demanding physical requirements, including running a two-mile course through the woods while carrying a seventy-five-pound backpack.

The women in the army study were not weight lifters or brawny marines. They were civilian students and others who had volunteered for a strength-training course. Many had never exercised before. Several were mothers who had recently given birth.

I wonder how much female strength is affected by our conviction that we can't—can't open the pickle jar, turn the compost, dig a ditch, or throw a ball. I still find myself mutely handing the splitting maul over to my boyfriend, assuming he can split more firewood. And he can, from a lifetime of practice.

In one thought-provoking experiment done some years ago, subjects were tested for strength after being exposed to suggestions of weakness or power. Following the suggestions of weakness, strength scores plummeted. Suggestions of greater strength increased the subjects' results. The authors concluded that psychological factors may play an important role in physical ability, which leads to the interesting question of how much women's strength is affected by constant reminders of weakness.

In my experience, it does seem men my size are slightly stronger. I don't know if this is the result of a lifetime of physical activity, biological differences, individual differences, training, or a combination of all these factors.

When I find myself thinking that men are hopelessly stronger, however, I remember my first real boxing match, against a woman who can punch harder than most men. And I think of some of the men at the gym who are decidedly weaker than I am.

The idea that women aren't as strong as men still has remarkable impact on our lives. Whether women feel safe walking to their car at night; whether men treat us patronizingly when we tackle physical tasks; whether women are welcome in jobs such as construction; whether girls are invited to join in when boys play—our lives are still defined by assumptions about our bodies.

Intrinsic to our understanding of what our bodies are capable of is what we think drives them. We have the notion that aggression is innately a male characteristic and not a female one: a ferocity that is the birthright for one sex—and unavailable to the other.

Once a trainer was telling me I had to *get more vicious,* and Jess interrupted him, shaking his head: "She isn't like that," he said under his breath.

Meaning, I'm a woman: a feminine looking woman with long hair and polite manners. Until recently, Jess had trouble recognizing that a woman could have that same core of aggression a man can have. He clearly believed that I am too sweet, too kind— too feminine and female—to be mean.

Later, Jess seemed to revise his views. I don't think he was motivated by any intellectual exercise, but rather, by seeing other women fight, and, perversely, by a feeling of protection: he didn't want me to get hurt. The axiom always rings true: The best defense is a good offense.

I think Jess also began to forget that I'm female. He started treating me as a fighter. Sometimes he would reach out, reflexively, to pat me on the behind, only to find his hand frozen inches away from my tush.

It's a scene, we are told, as old as mankind. A hulking caveman is standing near a fire. In one hand, he holds a club; in the other, a carcass of some sort. In front of the fire is a cavewoman—

111

cooking, of course. In her hands are not the instruments of the hunt, but those of domesticity. At any moment, he might drag her off by her hair.

The idea that men are biologically predestined to be more aggressive than women—the evolutionary result of a prehistoric past, genetically imprinted on the mind—has ongoing popularity, a theme played in endless reruns by popular culture.

It's an argument appealing for its simplicity, but on close appraisal, it's more like an old sweater full of little holes. Despite all the work of scientists to find the "criminal gene" and other efforts to name a biological reason for human aggression, none has ever been found.

The hormone testosterone, for instance, has proved impervious to efforts to prove it causes aggression. Researchers have found both sexes manufacture considerable quantities of the misnamed "male" and "female" hormones (the male body, for instance, is reliant upon estrogen for bone growth). The complex nature of these hormones makes it difficult to prove which is having what effect. Recent studies have suggested that if there is a hormonal influence to aggression, it may be *estrogen*. Adolescent girls given estrogen treatments for delayed puberty showed increased aggression; so do male mice given the hormone.

We are still far away from understanding precisely what role— if any—biology plays in behavior. Correlations have been found between high lead levels and extreme violence in children. Some disorders, such as schizophrenia, are also associated with the increased likelihood of violence, though most schizophrenics are nonviolent.

Yet the countless social factors to be considered—gun availability, absent parenting, schools, values—seem to offer more possibilities than purely biological explanations. Even in instances where physical factors may play a role, environment would appear to dictate the outcome. A schizophrenic individual who is given the proper medication and family support is going to behave differently from one who is deinstitutionalized and left homeless.

No single factor can explain aggression. When confronted with another bit of evidence shaking his theory, an author who claims that single parenting causes crime once complained that he was "getting that complexity feeling." To me, "that complexity feeling" seems unavoidable when discussing aggression.

Unfortunately, many writers seem anxious to avoid any complexity feeling, skating thinly over conflicting evidence in an effort to prove predestined differences between the sexes. To give just one example, in his book *The Red Queen: Sex and the Evolution of Human Nature,* writer Matt Ridley uses the statistic that ninety-three percent of drunken drivers in the United States are men as proof that male aggression cannot be explained by "social conditioning alone."

But in the decade between the publication of this statistic (1983) and the publication of Ridley's book (1993), the percentage of American women arrested for drunk driving nearly doubled. For me, this hints that gender differences with regard to drunk driving *are* due to social conditioning. The rising rates represent not evolutionary change but a simple increase in the number of women driving. As women drive more, the percentage who do so drunk will continue to rise.

The dismaying thing about biological approaches to aggression is that instead of exploring the topic of aggression, they focus on explaining it—quickly, and politically. That's the beauty of biopolitics: if you say something enough times, it becomes a matter of common sense. If you maintain that men are more aggressive, you cut all the evidence to the contrary off at the knees. Who wants to talk about women who drive when drunk? They simply don't do it.

I believe people have a *potential* for aggression—which is different from a *drive.* Aggression is like language. An infant can learn it, but it does not come programmed and pretaught (the nature of behavior always involves an element of invention). It is not inevitable or necessary that any of us act aggressively.

But while we are not driven to aggress, we all have the ability to do so. Each aggressive behavior is a potential that, depending on the situation, is nourished, dissuaded, or ignored by our communities and our families—sometimes directly, sometimes inadvertently.

Some of the fighters bring their children and wives to wait while they work out. There is one beautiful little girl with coffee-colored skin and eyelashes as fine as embroidery who boasts her own set of tiny boxing gloves. Dressed in a pinafore, church shoes, and boxing gloves, she followed me one day as I warmed up by throwing punches, mimicking my every move. I have a friend who tells me about another girl, her oldest daughter. The girl is obsessed with dresses and playing princess games. She won't leave the house unless she is dolled up to the nines. Her mother has bought her plenty of pants and rough-and-tumble toys, but the daughter isn't interested. Now the mother wonders if gender differences with respect to aggression are innate after all. Why else would her daughter end up wanting to dress like a princess every day?

Rather than being biologically determined, behavior may signify other socialization the child receives—from grandparents, neighbors, teachers—as well as subtleties in our own parenting that we aren't aware of. While parents may give their girls trucks to play with, not very many allow their little boys to dress up as fairy princesses and encourage them to put on mom's perfume. I believe biological assumptions allow us to avoid addressing the many ways we still treat boys and girls differently.

Some of us do learn to be nonaggressive when we are young. But early training can be rejected later, forgotten in moments of anger, decisively conquered, or dismissed behind closed doors.

In a famous 1963 Yale experiment in which college students were allowed to administer electric shocks to a victim, women showed themselves just as likely to aggress as men. In fact, the female students were more inclined to push the high-voltage button, and to keep their finger pressed on it, even as their victims gave tremendous cries of pain and distress.

Who knows where people's lives will lead? The potential for aggression remains, and the girl who plays fairy princess at age six may end up a rugby coach, a tough criminal lawyer, or even in prison.

Or she may end up like that little girl looking up at me as she secretly followed my steps, her black shoes clickity-clatting across the floor, a warm draft of air pillowing the yellow dress above her brown legs. Laughing, her father commented, "Now that's what I call shadowboxing."

One day, a young fighter came up to me, excitement in his eyes. He was maybe eighteen, with a tattooed, wiry frame and bristle-cut hair.

"Jess says I get to spar next week," he announced. I congratulated him. He added, "Jess said it was with a female, so I guess it's with you. I don't see any other females in here fighting."

I never react anymore, hearing myself referred to as "female," a strangely clinical word. I know no one means any ill by it. The men at the gym use it sometimes instead of a word like *woman* because it is more neutral. A *woman* is someone you may see romantically, but a *female* is just another aspect to a person, like her weight class. I appreciate the intent behind the word choice, the effort to place my gender aside, to make me into another fighter, who happens to be female.

I tried to make him feel at ease, mentioning I needed to work on my defense (unstated meaning: I won't hit you much). He nodded, agreeing. "You'll work on your defense, me on my offense, right?"

Then, eyeing my blocky shoulders, he added with sincerity and worry, "You'll take it easy on me, won't you?"

Not too long ago, I was asked if 1 believe women should be able to compete against men in the ring—for real, for titles. My response was immediate. Of course. Not just because women in boxing are marginalized by lack of competition but also because I believe that women can do it.

Maybe not this year, or even this decade, but someday, with the proper training from an early age, a woman could attain the skills needed to compete against men on the professional level—especially at the lower weight classes. The person who asked me (it happened on an English radio station, actually) seemed shocked at my answer, and he promptly began to bluster. What, he wanted to know, if women get hurt?

"Not us," I responded. "Them."

Perhaps that is the fear underlying so many of our beliefs in strength differences, in innate versus learned aggression, in the fair sex versus the strong. It's the fear that, given an opportunity, a woman matched against a man just might, as horrible as it sounds, beat the dickens out of him—that we will not take it so easy on men after all.

That kid never did come back in the gym to spar.

T'ai Chi Tales

Richard Grossinger

Plainfield, Vermont (1974)

In September, Andy and Carolyn, California nomads, arrived in Plainfield in hope of building solar houses. They had been studying t'ai chi ch'uan in Berkeley, and they demonstrated it at the Grange Hall—a version with rising and sinking motions (Anne mimicked it because I wasn't there). When she asked if they'd be willing to teach, they put her and Bob in charge.

I was, at best, equivocal. In 1974 t'ai chi was a strange exercise. True, my high-school companion Chuck had become an adept practitioner, apprenticing in Chinatown; but he was ahead on everything—tarot, yoga, and Beat poetry in the '60s; alchemy and Tibetan Buddhism in the '70s—and it had always seemed hopeless (and base ambition) to want to catch up. He had carried out duels with a wooden sword and, while visiting us earlier in the summer, had—pot-belly, beard, and all—hopped from stone to stone in the Winooski River.

On the night of the first class, Barre's main street was a thoroughfare of shopping. I dawdled stair by stair but arrived anyway at the room on the second floor of the dilapidated storefront. There, behind the blue-orange neon of KARATE, I found a place among milling men and women. Without warning, Andy and Carolyn began, arms extending, then drawn back, hands rolling, feet shifting in tight arcs. He was dark, medium height, a pixie; she was tall and fair, stylish. His arms worked shuttles; her fingertips trickled out like spider threads.

As directed, twenty or so of us got arranged in three rows. Andy addressed us. "Leave your hang-ups outside," he pointed at the window. "If they're that interesting you can pick them up on your way out." His tinge of wit got my attention. "Find your axis—that's the line of gravity through the top of your head clear down to the balls of your feet—it's the thing that holds you to the earth." He paused to allow us to picture this. "Now follow me."

I encountered memories of Y rooms—smell of Hershey bars, radiator pipes, woolen sweaters piled in the corner. Herded inside on rainy days, we would be guided in knee-bends, jumping jacks, and other drills of strength and coordination. I was ever out of synch. Right and left would be confused, then front and rear, up and down.

"Find your center," Andy called out. "Move it toward your spine." Did he mean a spot inside me?

"Keep the circle soft. Even if it hurts more to do it that way you learn where the tension comes from. You guide the healing process."

'What if I don't have a center?' I wondered. There was no core-like spot X-rayed in my body-mind.

He and Carolyn were so lovely—if only we could just be them.

That Sunday, above the village at the edge of an apple grove, they stood beside each other. For over an hour they synchronized 106 moves, motionless motion. Their precision transfused an image I kept coming back to; it sustained me in the class while one by one the more precocious students dropped out until, a month later, surprisingly only eight of us remained.

Plainfield, Vermont (1974)

The t'ai chi class is down to five: me, Anne, Bob, Eugenie, and Viuu. Two evenings a week we go through the form up to where we last learned; then Andy teaches a new move. We practice it. Then he and Carolyn correct our renditions. Then we review the sequence to that point.

Afterwards Eugenie and I do the two-person form, called push-hands. My palm rests on her ward-off (her arm in the shape of "an empty embrace"). The rotation of my waist launches a strike she deflects into her center. She turns without breaking the axis of her spine so that her ward-off automatically becomes an attack and my striking hand curls into its own ward-off as I roll back. One part of me is trying to imagine myself inside the mystery, carrying a ball of Taoist energy; another part knows there is no ball and I am an imperfect mimic of an external form.

At home I stand in the precise center of the living room and go through the motions—Grasp Sparrow's Tail, strike, Embrace Tiger, Step Back like a Monkey, Put a Needle at Sea-Bottom, Spread Arms like a Fan, Descend like a Snake. I raise up on one leg, hand floating to eye level . . . White Crane Becoming Brush Knee, twist step.

My life is no longer just a mythology. I am writing me.

Berkeley, California (1975)

The second night after I arrived in Berkeley in the summer of 1975 I dialed the number Carolyn had handed me in Vermont. The woman answering did not seem to know either her or Andy, but stated brusquely, "Yes, t'ai chi meets in my yard—7:00 on Tuesday and Thursday evenings and six mornings a week. No class on Saturday."

"Is Paul still teaching?"

"We study t'ai chi. Whoever comes participates. My name is Carol. It's my house. I'm the instructor."

My instructions were to park on McKinley and come down the driveway. As I ducked through brambles, I suddenly saw it, a Brueghel t'ai chi classic, vivid in every detail: a lemon tree, a cat prowling, people in pairs. I stood respectfully and (I hoped) unobtrusively by the side.

The participants included one very large, elegantly dressed woman, a man in overalls, two women in a corner pushing together, a dark-haired Indian-looking woman, and a storklike man with glasses pushing forcefully against a squat, red-haired man. There were ten women, four men, and all seemed very adept. The red-haired man might have been straining, but I wasn't advanced enough to tell if he was rigid and immobile or grounded and strong.

I recognized Paul from Andy's depiction. Pushing with one of the women, he was a tall reed with a pale, oval face. Strands of light brown hair fell over his ears and forehead. About my age, he wore a shapeless white robe. Even as I noticed him, he acknowledged my presence by a smile.

Finally he bowed to his partner and walked over. "You must have come from Vermont," he remarked pleasantly.

I assumed Carol had told him about my call, but just to be sure, I brought regards from my teachers.

"Carolyn was wonderful," he interrupted at the mere mention of her name. "She learned to be so much softer."

I told him I knew the set but wasn't very good.

He asked about the drive out West, then what I was doing in Vermont.

I felt childlike excitement. Paul wasn't just a student or teacher, or even a poet. He wasn't a Vermont apparatchik. He was one of the mythical California people who had lived through the Summer of Love. He seemed archangelic standing there, nodding approvingly as I overanswered while trying to be spare. He just kept smiling and asking more questions, chatting away about everything from the origin of the Great Salt Lake to what kinds of books I wrote.

"But I shouldn't be keeping you from the class," I finally inserted, for it was proceeding without us.

He gazed at me through cosmically blue eyes or, more accurately, at a point slightly above me. "You're not keeping me from t'ai chi. We're *doing* t'ai chi. You're sending energy, and I'm giving it back. Talk is a very powerful form of t'ai chi. Very subtle, very wonderful. You give energy. You yield." He turned to his left as if to cycle my words. "It's all the same principles." Then, without warning, he raised his right ward-off for my hands. He was utterly weightless; I felt like a heavy ball bearing. He rotated from his waist in an arc. I tried to relax and let his movement transfer itself to me. He was so willowy and supple it was a more complicated orbit than I had experienced with anyone before—wider, emptier, spiraling.

Sightseeing no longer, I had fallen from an amateur field in Vermont to a backyard of savants. Paul's hand probed for my center; my palm slid along the hairs of his arm, measuring his shifting arc. Lemon blossoms released oils in the dusk.

A pleasant ache shot up my spine and expanded at my shoulder blades. Was this his potent *ch'i* or my over-fervent imagination? Either way I was trapped by his push. He smiled in recognition, released me, and began again.

"Don't be in such a hurry," he offered. "There's no reason to do it faster or slower. We have time. In fact, we have nothing *but* time."

121

During the next cycle he departed from the form as I knew it, yanking my arm abruptly back and holding it. When I didn't know what to do, he twisted it so that I was forced to turn, then coiled a fist into my shoulder blade. As I resisted, he gave a light slap to my face, forcing me to respond upward with my ward-off.

Complimenting me on my quick improvement, he said, "You should work with Doris." He traded me with one of the women in the pair closest to us.

Suddenly I was exchanging circles with a nereid in a pillowy white dress, a flower in her hair, too-sweet perfume. The adjustment was like dropping off a cliff. Her presence was so vacant the hand she offered was not there. She caught me at once in her ward-off. The moment I rotated back she tugged me over to show how much I was leaning. We began again, my hand directed just inside her bracelet, our beachball rolling back and forth, one part of my mind trying to decide if she was pretty, her face remote and expressionless.

After push-hands, Paul and Carol demonstrated a series that included Step Back Like a Monkey, Embrace Tiger/Return to Mountain, and Move Hands like a Cloud. They were dramatic, powerful partners—he a quick cat, pouncing back and forth; she whirling emphatically around him and striking swordlike—he suddenly behind her; she suddenly behind him. I knew the moves from Vermont, but the nuances they added made them seem totally novel.

We split into pairs and practiced this sequence over and over as they came around, inserting themselves and correcting.

It was past eight when Paul assembled us to do the set. As fog cooled my sweat, shape turned into shape, in me and around me. I felt how perfect this was, silently synchronized. Then the teacher bowed to the departing students, one by one.

There was no word of when Paul's last class would be, but he kept warning that one of these days he'd be gone. I was trying to learn as much as possible in the brief time we had, staying after class and practicing with him and Carol. We did a free-form version of push-hands, adhering to each other as we pursued through the yard, a hand to an arm, a finger to a shoulder, a forearm to a flank, trying to sense energy and respond to a partner's unpredictable darts and feints. I imagined the energy ball as a luminous version of the orb I had chased all my life. Yet this was wild and elating in a whole new way.

Before meeting Paul and Carol I wouldn't have thought myself austere, but something in me balked at the sinuosity of their circles, at reaching out and touching someone's chest, or bending low and twisting up without self-consciousness. These shapes weren't yet part of me.

Every step of Paul's and Carol's, even when not doing t'ai chi, was conscious and soft. I moved among them as a clubfoot, concealing embarrassment in innocence. But embarrassment for what? Doing it poorly, or doing it at all?

Over the month Paul taught me the moves of a two-person set called *san shou,* which matched partners in a formalized sequence of strikes, slaps, kicks, and their neutralizations. Even though I was a beginner doing an advanced practice, his method was simply to place me opposite him and begin; I followed as best I could. When I blanked out or was in the wrong place he dislodged me (or simply stopped). Then we started over.

Eyes sparkling, face ever quixotic, Paul led me to California jolt by jolt. His calm words belied the forcefulness of his gestures. "I'm trying to get your attention," he explained. "If you won't give it to me, you encounter my energy before you're ready for it. I could *tell* you the same thing but you're so used to words you wouldn't bother to listen."

"It's not a fight," he preached one morning during class. "You're all trying too hard to knock each other over."

123

He summoned Doris to the head of the yard. "Attack me," he challenged.

Emboldened, she gave a hard push followed by a sharp press. Casually he stepped aside and she stumbled.

"Come on, Doris, really attack me!"

She charged at him, back and forth like a cartoon of an enraged bull. Each time, he pivoted away and guided her into a fall. She was amused but exasperated; she wanted to smash him.

"If you knock me over, Doris, that would only be because you gave me too much energy before I was ready to ... *receive it,*" stepping aside and pulling her down at the word 'receive.' "When I'm ready, your energy is a gift." He spun as her glancing blow fluttered into space.

She came at him this time like a wild creature, both arms thrashing, swinging for his face.

"Those are presents, little presents of your energy. I'm honored you want to give me so much without getting any ... baaaack." He whirled and immobilized her, bending her arm behind her. "This is a dangerous position," he demonstrated to our merriment as Doris added grimaces for comic effect. "But dangerous also means healthy. Bend-Bow Shoot-Tiger activates an acupuncture point." He jiggled her to show the meridian. "When we do the move we give our partner a treatment. If we're skillful they appreciate it." Doris verified this with a strained grin. "You can't help but heal your opponent. That's the nature of the *tao.*"

At the end of class he led us through the first section of the set, so slowly it was almost unendurable, each movement infinitesimally changing into the next, our bodies rising and sinking. An hour instead of fifteen minutes.

Then he announced he was leaving for Idaho at the end of the week.

In the final meeting Paul proceeded as usual, dissecting moves, he and Carol observing, correcting. "We could just hit," he told one pair, "but that wouldn't be subtle enough; it wouldn't be t'ai chi. There would be nothing in reserve." He chuckled at his own conceit and stared at clouds as though parodying the ethereal savant. Lemon flowers sparkled among lemons, and next door someone was hanging a paisley on a clothesline. "Everyone talks about not having enough energy. But there's plenty of energy, all around." He demonstrated, making soft lotuses in the air. "They don't want it." He shook his head in astonishment: "They *just don't want it!*"

He was still weaving this paradigm as he moved to the next pair: "It's like massage. The most powerful massage of all is not Rolfing. It's the massage where you are not even touching. That's the most subtle but also the most profound. The fingers move above the body, activating points. That's the style that takes the longest to learn."

He set himself before me and offered a ward-off. "No past or future," he chided as I rushed through the move I thought I knew to get to the move he was teaching. "There are no simple moves or hard moves. If you hurry through ward-off left to get to fist under elbow you never get to fist under elbow. Everything is changing in all parts all the time. You can add tension to it, but you can't arrive any faster."

"Why?" he asked the class. "Why the resistance? Why be anxious to leave the moment you get there?"

As we practiced strikes, he instructed: "Right hand creeping by the ear, sensing. Heisenberg's Principle of Uncertainty."

"Bullshit," shouted Jeff, jock auto-mechanic in Adidas, usually his biggest admirer.

Paul looked hurt.

"You tell me how it's some Heisenberg Principle of Uncertainty!"

"You really want to know, do you?"

Jeff nodded.

"Well," Paul mused, completing the spiral of his strike, "the movement is continuous; there's no break move to move, no moment when everything isn't changing—it's a wave. But each moment is discrete; each moment some new exchange is beginning; each moment needs absolute attention—it's a particle. You can't break the wave to hold the particle. And you can't give up the particle to form the wave."

At the end of class he reminded us to open our joints and let *ch'i* flow. "If you don't feel it, don't worry, just keep doing it. Pretend you're feeling it. That's better than pretending you're *not* feeling it. At least you're establishing a lifelong relationship to t'ai chi."

Everyone left him a gift. Mine was a copy of my book *The Slag of Creation* fresh from the printer. Carol presented a loaf of bread, Doris a t'ai chi shirt, Jeff was going to repair his car for the trip.

One morning Carol told me to try pushing hands with my eyes shut. "Remove the distraction. Don't worry about correctness. See if you can *feel* what I'm trying to show you. Not through your head—through your body."

I closed my eyes. All at once her cycle became palpable. Even as I stumbled in darkness, I felt each ripple of her changing pressure, though after several minutes, my arms grew weary. I was sure she would stop. But we went more rapidly, our hands tracing an infinity symbol, my shoulder blades aching unbearably.

"Good," she urged, "you're getting closer. Don't stop now."

I encountered a failure my whole time on Earth to keep at something that wasn't hedged against an image of what I was going to do next, by a fantasy of who I was or what women were presently attractive to me, or my planned flight home where I could sink into the nullity of my life. Carol was how I imagined

California people who are advanced. She strolled from dawn meditation to morning class. Her sombrero kept direct sun off her. She was a paragon of strictness, lacking Paul's spirit of mischief. In addition to t'ai chi, she instructed me on diet and herbs. She was openly shocked that I ate at pancake and hamburger houses and bought canned foods. She blamed most of my t'ai chi failings on these practices.

(Her sentiment was reinforced by a man with a turban in Dana Ullman's class. When we graduated to taking each other's cases, my main complaint was upset stomachs, so he asked me what foods made me sick.

"I don't know."

"How little consciousness you show," he retorted pompously, "just stuffing things inside of yourself with no attention to what they are and how they change you—let alone their karma.")

Finally Carol said I could open my eyes. Waves of light trembled against me. She looked so different, her sullen face that of an old shaman, her sombrero and scarf representing her attachment to perfection.

Suddenly my arms were effortless. They began to move by themselves. Extending from my body, they traced a globe of multidimensional spheres, flowing into, out of, and penetrating one another. My thinking had stopped.

Carol slid her arm away. We bowed to each other. Class was over.

When Carol told me that Paul was enjoying my book, I pictured him on the edge of the northern wilderness, leading a class much like Andy and Carolyn's. "Is he happy in Idaho?" I asked.

A Paul-like smile crept over her face. "He hasn't gone anywhere."

I was bewildered. "He's still on Woolsey Street. Why don't you go visit him. He'd like to see you."

127

It never occurred to me he would say good-bye and then not depart.

Driving across the Oakland border, I parked on a block of large, rundown houses, all divided (as was evident from the mailboxes) into four or five apartments. A flight of outdoor stairs like a fire escape led to Paul's rooms at the top of a three-story Victorian. I had called ahead, so he was waiting on the landing, perched over a map of Idaho. He quickly answered my unspoken question:

"I haven't left because I haven't decided where I want to go. I can leave any time. That's not a problem. I can leave right now, in fact. But right now I'm studying this map."

His hand was moving so the parchment beneath it seemed a kind of alchemical document, different colors for roads, lakes, mountains—the joints, veins, arteries, and skin of the earth, he explained. His fingers wriggled along meridians—the big one, the Salmon, and then Lost River, Birch Creek, North Fork. He pointed out Pocatello.

"This is where I grew up. Atom-bomb country. Those of us who've come from there have had to learn to heal ourselves."

He dowsed further north. "There's a high-energy area around Coeur d'Alene. That's where I'm going. I don't know anyone there yet, but there's probably a woman who's studied properties of local herbs. I'll find her. She'll find me." Berkeley sun glistened on Pend Oreille and the Coeur d'Alene Lakes. "Maybe there's a place I can practice acupuncture. I'm going to do acupuncture of the Earth. Do you realize that every time you dig with a shovel it's putting in a needle and opening a flow?"

We passed through the doorway to his kitchen. Although robust, Paul had a wan, ephemeral quality about him, like a Celtic Christ. Along shelves were fibrous herbs and powders in jars. This was a Mediaeval apothecary—no sign anywhere of commercial America.

"Our culture has a protein obsession," he observed. "But we make all we need. And if we let ourselves make it instead of having it made for us we are stronger internally, though maybe not as strong on the outside. We exist closer to the way plants do. We are more sensitive to light, to *ch'i*." He undulated his hand in rays through glass. There was a decanter on the table. "It's water," he explained. "But water left in sun changes."

We crossed into the living room. I refused a glass of the water because, ever fastidious, I felt a need to protect myself from weirdness.

He explained how he lived here once with a woman named Janet. "In fact, she left only a few days ago."

This was a surprise to me and implied a more mundane reason for the end of the class. "She used to be married," he added. "In fact, she *is* married; she still has a husband back in Virginia. She went to see him."

I was at once concerned to know whether she was going to Idaho too.

"No, I don't expect her back; I've become too subtle for her. I had a dream last night about her husband. He was driving a car, pretending to be going real fast, but he had a flat tire. I asked him why he didn't change the tire. Then I realized—he didn't have a spare. And he didn't know he didn't have a spare. He didn't even know the tire was flat."

I smiled despite myself.

"I can't say he's in a bad place," he mused, continuing to talk about Janet's husband rather than Janet. "After all, that's where he is. He chose to be there, right? But he's ill-equipped. He's trying to go seventy. First he should slow down. He should stop right where he is and do something about a spare tire. We all should. That's what t'ai chi is for. T'ai chi gives energy in reserve."

I wondered aloud if Paul was evading his emotions from the breakup of the relationship.

"Psychology is an obsession of this culture, like protein. It might be this thing that happened or that. Who knows? Right now there is only all the energy at our disposal. It doesn't matter where it comes from—genetics, trauma, the stars. We get to use it all the same."

I returned two mornings later and we pushed hands in his yard. In the heat of the sun I was mesmerized by his spirals, pleased by the honor of his company. Then—the summer-long trick—his arm came from nowhere, caught my reverie in a lock, and twisted me ruggedly to the ground.

"There's no break in t'ai chi," he said. "There's no time you can allow your attention to rise into your head like that." I stood and reengaged. He found my frozen point and threw me again.

I knew I couldn't meet him. My whole life of Grossinger's, baseball, college teaching, and literary symbolism stood in the way. His harshness had broken through the scenery and shattered my romanticism.

He suggested we do the mirror image of the set, side by side.

"Step back like a monkey!" he shouted. The Ba Kua fish had leapt from the water through the ripples of my encircling ward-off. Its hand now sank to form a fist under my elbow, punctuating its leap. "Like a monkey," he hailed, arms sagging monkey-like. Suddenly we were distracted by children reaching to pick carrots. "Don't do that," Paul called out. "Somebody was taking care of those, waiting for them to grow."

They stepped back, surveying us worriedly.

"You have wonderful floppy ears," he told the girl.

"I have ears like a monkey," she said.

"That's right!" Paul howled. "We're monkeys." And to their astonishment we flew back into the move together.

Afterwards in the kitchen I accepted a cup of flax tea from sun water. "When will you go?" I asked him.

"Parts of me are going now. I'm moving slowly. There are lots of ways to leave fast if that's what I want to do." He pointed to the map. "Airports here … here … here … here." Each one a little black plane. "I can hitch. I can drive the car Janet left behind." He peered out the window. It was a tan VW Bug. "It's not a question of my getting there. It's a matter of waiting here as long as I can, until I'm perfectly ready. My mind is almost there. You only see what's left of me. But if I hadn't left this part behind we wouldn't have been able to talk and learn about each other."

Then he announced, to my horror, that we were approaching the day of the next San Andreas earthquake. "First the Pyramid will be built," he declared. "That's what Edgar Cayce said. Then the earthquake will follow."

I knew, if there was such a prophecy, that Transamerica had already fulfilled the first half of it, and I wondered, with blatantly egoic concern, if we would get out in time.

"Sure," he said. "The abbot will leave the temple in San Francisco. That will be the sign."

I asked if he would go then. "Maybe. If I make it, I do. If I don't, I don't. The earthquake comes. Or it doesn't come. We're here. We're not here. It's all the same, life or death. The cosmic circle. We can't run. We can't hurry. It's going to come out the same either way."

Plainfield, Vermont (1975)

T'ai chi class, pumpkin field, Carolyn and Andy leading. While we wait in *wu chi*, all the background comes alive—mauve of sky, din of crickets, mountain mist.

The moves begin. In their singleness I feel I have learned nothing.

A toad's golden eyes look up at me from the grass. They do not see me.

I feel a mark that begins at my forehead, splits my eyes but is neither a crevice nor a series of cracks. It plummets down my chest with thousands of filaments and rootlets, each a breath, each a mineral. It will never be uprooted. I cannot uproot it.

San Francisco (1978)

That fall, with Carol's class down to two people, I decided to seek out the legendary master Benjamin Pang Jeng Lo, a disciple of the late Cheng Man-ch'ing. Once I found him (among the countless Lo's in the San Francisco phone book) I paid two months' tuition and joined the 6 AM Bay Bridge rush. Soon I had to wake even earlier to make it all the way to his new storefront on Clement Avenue near the ocean.

It was the end of backyard free form. On a cold stone floor I practiced a spare and rigorous set. Arriving bleary-eyed, often in rain, I tried to concentrate on Ben's painful corrections. After each move, class members held their postures for examination. I froze in place, legs shaking, waiting for the master to make his way around the room to adjust me ... to twist my back and downward-aimed punch into something I had to spring up from in pain a second later. He repeated pet homilies of encouragement: "It hurt, that good—very good!" and "No see mistake, no correct. First see, then correct." ("I'll do it someday," I'd think. "It's great stuff. Just don't make me do it today.")

Oakland, California (1991–2)

T'ai chi had become a Taoist puzzle for me, the same silent moves year after year, at which I remained an eternal beginner. In 1983 I stopped going to class. For the next seven years I practiced only sporadically. I forgot most of the set.

Then in January, 1991, I drove up the coast to Garberville where Paul Pitchford was starting a Chinese medicine clinic at Heartwood Institute. That night, as we toted our vegetarian banquet trays to a corner in the community center, I asked the recent émigré from Idaho a question about beets and algae. "The best food for you," he teased, "would be to rise at 6 AM tomorrow morning for my t'ai chi class."

I promised to try.

Outside the *kiva,* fog burying the sun's attempt to rise and minimally warm us, Paul corrected my rusty set. He also offered a piece of advice. As I considered aloud whether to go back to Martin Inn's Oakland group, he joked, "Why don't you study with a real world champion. At least you'll learn to fight."

It was a typical Pitchford ploy, to advance the antithesis of what he purportedly believed.

Peter Ralston was a new author of ours who ran the infamously combative Cheng Hsin School of Ontology and Martial Arts only a few blocks west of my home. He was World Champion (or so the sign above his storefront proclaimed, for he had won some tournament in Taipei in 1978). This declamation—a landmark of Telegraph Avenue kitsch—had led me to reject a manuscript he kept submitting going back to our Richmond days. World champion of what?

Paul had trained with Ralston in the early '70s; then they had gone their separate ways—Paul into herbs and ritual Buddhism, Peter into Zen and samurai training.

Cheng Hsin apprentices kept bringing their master's book back to me at approximately three-year intervals. Their patience paid off. I had snobbily limited our t'ai chi fare to the elite lineage of Ben Lo and Cheng Man-ch'ing, but we needed new territory, even if it offended our purist colleagues. American—lingo warrior arts were a perfect item for chain bookstores—t'ai chi in Tae Kwon Do robes.

Joining his class, I soon found Peter to be a Heidegger of combat, a pragmatic street fighter who threw aside homage to traditional form and reinvented moves solely to suit function. He had won his fabled Taiwan match by scientific fighting. He meant to drown out, frustrate, and negate all formal sets, macho propagandas, psychospiritual pieties, and *ch'i* myths students brought along. His intention was to provide four walls, a floor, mirrors, training partners, and a riddle. Cheng Hsin was the premier school of phenomenology and martial arts.

"Correction is about changing *whatever* is not effective," the World Champion announced at the opening meeting of "Principles of Effortless Power." "My only question is: does it work? I don't want to reject tradition to make another superficial system." A balding pugilist with a fierce jovial stare, he spun, lotus-kicked, and struck an invisible target with both fists before a mirror reflecting another mirror—an infinite regression of tigers. "Begin with who you are, what your actual experience is, your fears and fantasies." He halted and faced us, a group comprised mostly of eager young testosteroned males (Martin's class was primarily women). "When you're in line to ride the roller coaster, most of your problem is concept. What you fear isn't what comes up once you're *on* the roller coaster. It's all in your mind. Get it? The real thing, not the fear! If you had to fight Muhammad Ali in his prime, you might think your lack of boxing skill would be your greatest problem. But getting into that ring, feeling the energy of the crowd— just being in that situation would defeat you before you began."

So "principles of effortless power" meant measuring steps with the precision of a surveyor, aligning with gravity, feeling an opponent's energy before he moved, retraining one's own predisposition to act in an habitual manner.

I abandoned my set and began anew. I walked on invisible posts above an ocean. I measured steps in half-inches, the placement of my feet in degrees. I gauged a plumb line dropping through my head into the "bubbling wells" of my soles. I pretended not knowing if the wall existed. Then I did push-hands with the wall.

By feeling what it was like to be a water droplet I became a human droplet.

I stood face to face with a bellicose jock who, without making physical contact, tried to terrify me with gestures. I remained calm and deflected his force.

I wandered around the room with my eyes closed, hands extended, sensing energy fields of my classmates so I wouldn't bump into them.

"Accept what is, or may be, always as the first step. Adhere to activity and observe the requirements for an advantageous position." These were Peter's mottos.

"I'm here and you're there," he announced one day. "I'm here and you're there. I'm here and you're there. This is the single most profound thing. You think you hear me, but you don't. I'm here and you're there." He took a step and pointed. "Every inch between us is conscious. I'm here and you're there. I'm going to keep repeating it until you get it. I'm *here* and you're *there.*"

"We might think we want utopia," he told us another time, "but there is no place in it for us. It wouldn't work. It would break down in a relatively short time. I wouldn't even give it a year. Because you see, we wouldn't be there. We don't have the discipline for something like that. We don't have the courage, the persistence, the overwhelming courage it takes for something like that. In fact, you want to go there *so you don't have to be courageous.* Right? You want to go there so you can get away from this!"

Every Saturday, Cheng Hsin held free practice for all students, past and present, so after breakfast I would ride my bike to the dojo and hang around for training. One such morning I made the acquaintance of Ron Sieh, an original Ralston apostle who had helped Peter train for the W.C. (as insiders referred to it).

He was a small, wiry guy, about forty, incredibly fast, long stringy hair, movements like a hawk and a snake. He was show-ing off, refusing to acknowledge anyone's presence, taking big leaping kicks and shouting, "Yówee!" I thought he was prankishly blocking the mirror as I was trying to correct my set. After stew-ing about this for a moment, I broke the tension by asking him a question about the form. "I'm too advanced for you," he growled . . . and went on kicking.

I hated him. Yet there was something irresistible. He reminded me of my college buddy Schuyler. His persona was part Bruce Lee, part Peter Pan.

I knew I was going to ask him to be my teacher.

We met on Tuesday for lunch.

He said, "I'll teach you as long as you interest me."

So we began practicing together an hour a week at my house on the wooden floor above the pool. A disciple of both Vipassana and boxing, Ron trained mostly being present, paying attention, "filling the mind's holes," he called it.

"This isn't just mechanics and footwork," he reminded me, as we sparred in free form, "although you've got a problem there too. It's about spirit. *You need to find your spirit.* You're thinking too much, not seeing the world as it is. Do you ever *truly* realize that there is just as much space behind you as in front of you? I *know* you don't feel your back. Guy, you're not a puppet. Your roots go down beneath the earth. I bet you don't feel your feet, let alone what's under them. Make spikes under the ground. Shoot photon torpedoes! Put all that nervous energy down there. Be creative."

One afternoon in the warehouse Ron was mocking how I never really punched, how I didn't put commitment behind my strikes. "That's a girl's fist," he singsonged. "You know what happens when you punch like this?" He smacked his fist into his palm. "Crack! Broken bones!" He laughed.

We tried again. He was goading me to come back at him. Whenever I moved—no matter how quickly—he was faster, and tagged me.

"Zap!" he shouted. "Nailed again, big buddy! I'm trying to get you to be the best you can, but you obviously have some other agenda."

He was aiming to make me furious . . . and succeeding.

"You're locked in this limited image of what you're doing. Some weird little fantasy of winning perhaps?"

He began to jab harder, shouting things like "Dangerous art!" and "This is real!" dancing like Rocky, putting on a white-trash game face. As I executed a circle, punch, and kick, he faked terror, ducked, and called out, "Your body has some skill, but your mind is *all* fucked up!"

He had captured my spirit of play, my sense of the absurd. I came back at him like Ali in Zaire. Suddenly we stood toe to toe, throwing real punches—jabs and hooks. "Bob," he shouted. "Take your head out of the way—duh! Don't squeeze your thumb in your fist, you dope. You'll break your thumb. That's it. Keep going. Just because you made a nice move is no excuse to drop your guard." Mimicking a Roadrunner cartoon, he pointed at the ceiling, then laid a soft punch on my nose.

"Every time you let something slide by into unconsciousness, you're doing that. And we're practicing something else."

I moved more quickly, dancing around him, trying out the *hsing-i* Snake and Dove he had taught me. With amusement Ron neutralized them, then knocked me over hard. "Faster is not the issue. Timing is the issue. Stay in control. Hands out, dude! Move your left foot. No, your other left foot." I giggled and sighed. "Don't have a plan. When you think my punch is dead, I bend my elbow and turn it into a hook. Do the same. Render my actions obsolete by *your* actions." I took a step behind him, grabbed his arm, and attempted a version of Bend Bow, Shoot Tiger. For a moment we were stuck in place. Then I dislodged him and threw him stumbling in the other direction.

"Was that pure muscle or mystical will power?" he asked. "Did I detect Shoot Tiger?"

I nodded.

"You don't want to fight strength with strength. You don't want to make winning your goal. Remember Cheng Man-ch'ing: invest in loss. What did Bira call it: "playing in the mind"?

He pranced, darted, and rolled his hands in a spiraling ball. "Today I'm going to be," his voice changed to a cadent hush, "the cloud man."

Our exchange became swift and coordinated. For a minute I fantasized I was matching him. I wasn't flailing; I was corkscrewing out of the ground. He was backing up, and I was connecting. I couldn't stop grinning like a kid.

"You're doing great. But don't get hypnotized by the drama. Stay sober."

Then he called out, "Truce," and we fell down together laughing.

"Now that's fighting with spirit," he pronounced, grabbing my shoulders and shaking me as we headed outside. "But you have to throw your punches in one piece, from the earth through your hips down your forearm. There's still too much parasitic motion. The goal isn't activity. The goal is awareness. You want to die awake, to realize your last breath as your last breath."

Filipino Fighting Arts

Jeff Finder

Part 1: The Historical Setting

Southeast Asia: the words alone conjure up images of thickly covered verdant jungles, flowing across the hilltops to meet deeply shining blue seas. From time immemorial, this is a land that has been shrouded in mystery. Beneath the jungle's canopy lie many secrets—of spices, herbs, and precious gems. Countless men have died trying to wrest these treasures from their hidden places, and many more trying to protect them. Even the sea lanes have been guarded and defended, for along them have traveled the riches of several continents. Eventually these lands have given up their secrets, but among the last of these secrets has been the warrior skills that have defended these territories for centuries.

Human settlement throughout much of this vast region has been limited to very specific localities, separated from each other by hazardous terrain and by equally treacherous waters. Successive migratory waves have layered these lands with many competing ethnic groups, culturally and linguistically distinct from each other and often hostile to their closest neighbors.

Nowhere are these conditions more apparent than in the Philippines, an archipelago of over 7,000 islands stretching nearly 1,000 miles. Located between five and twenty degrees latitude north of the equator, at the juncture of the South Pacific and the South China Sea, and surrounded by smaller seas such as the Celebes and Sulu, the "Pearl of the Orient" has long been one of the world's great seafaring crossroads—a tropical realm of beauty and bloodshed.

Geographically, the Philippines is divided into three main regions. Luzon and Mindanao are the two great islands to the north and south, respectively; in the middle is the Visayas, a region of countless smaller islands. Only a third of the islands in the Philippines are inhabited, yet there are perhaps 700 different languages and dialects; sometimes neighboring villages cannot even converse with each other, speaking not just different dialects, but entirely different root languages.

The isolation of many villages and clans, separated from each other by the sea and further insulated by jungle and difficult terrain, has created an environment of virtually perpetual small-scale guerrilla warfare in which the struggle for survival rewards the strong. Both land and sea swallow the tracks of raiders, pirates, and bandits. In such an environment, it is incumbent upon all to learn to defend themselves or risk falling prey.

The earliest known inhabitants of the Philippines were small, dark-skinned people known as Negritos who came to the region in the distant past. About 5,000 years ago they were forced inland in order to survive the onslaught of the next immigrants, the Indo-Australians. The Indo-Australians in turn succumbed to successive waves of the fiercer and more advanced Mongoloid-Malayan race, starting around 100 BC. Each group that gave way was pushed back into rougher, more remote terrain that could more easily be defended. In the end this created an ethnic mosaic of mortal enemies across the land.

While the first immigrants are thought to have arrived by way of land bridges, now long since submerged, from Taiwan to the north and Borneo to the south, most inhabitants came by sea. The Malays in particular carried a superb tradition of sailing, having traversed the globe long before European explorers dared leave sight of land. Beginning about the tenth century AD, Filipino seafarers left their mark from Africa to China, and possibly even the shores of South America. Traders, adventurers, pirates, and slavers, they left evidence of their travels across two-thirds of the globe.

The Philippines were hardly unknown prior to their "discovery" by the Spanish in 1521. The oldest legends come from the stories of Sinbad, which mention Mindanao and Sulu, and it is possible that the ancient Egyptian writer Ptolemy knew of the Philippines as the Maniola Islands. The Chinese wrote of them as early as the third century AD and were trading with them by the fifth century. Soon thereafter the Philippines came under the influence of the Hindu Sri Vishayan Empire, which invaded from the mainland through Sumatra and then Borneo. The early fourteenth century saw the Javanese Madjapahit Empire wrest control from the Sri Vishaya.

Most of this early history of the Philippines is strictly oriental, having only sporadic contact with Europeans. Marco Polo spent several months in Sumatra and the surrounding region in 1292, waiting for favorable weather in order to escort a royal bride from the court of Kublai Khan to the King of Persia. There are even legends from the southern Philippines that trace royal Moro lineages back to Alexander the Great whose conquests extended well into India. While the Philippines were largely unknown to the people of the West, the reverse was certainly not true!

Part 2: The Art

While the first inhabitants of the islands undoubtedly had weapons and fighting skills for hunting and survival, the Filipino legend of the arrival of the art of kali begins during the waning days of the Sri Vishayan Empire in the late thirteenth century. Ten *datus,* or chiefs, fled from Borneo to the island of Panay in the western Visayas. Among their cultural contributions (which included laws, an alphabet, and weights and measures) was kali, an already ancient system of martial arts based on the sword. Kali is often used to refer to the "mother art" that existed before the myriad of styles now found across Southeast Asia. Some believe the word refers to the sword itself, called a *kalis.* Others say the term goes back even further, through Hindu influence to India and the ancient cult of the goddess Kali, who is always depicted with a sword in hand. As far away as Africa the word kali means "fierce," certainly a quality ascribed to the warrior followers of the Black Goddess.

The original art has grown and evolved into a myriad of styles, known by a variety of names. Besides kali, the two most well-known terms are escrima and arnis. Both of these terms come from the Spanish. Escrima, used mostly in the central Visayas, means "to fence" and is also imbued with the meaning "to skirmish," while arnis, the more common term currently used throughout the Philippines, refers to the "harness" a swordfighter would wear to carry his weapons.

No matter what the name, several dominant characteristics stand out about the Filipino martial arts (FMA). Above all, they are pragmatic. These are fighting systems first, arts second. As such, they are eminently practical, discarding pretty moves in favor of a solid theoretical framework and simple, useful drills based on combat experience.

Weapons are featured in FMA to a greater extent than in almost any other martial arts. The FMA are unusual in that they teach weapons first and foremost. They are thus more traditional than better-known self-defense systems such as karate, which teaches empty-hand techniques first and saves weapons for the practice of their senior disciples. Such arts were designed to meet the needs of societies emerging into the modern era. The Filipino arts, however, have not compromised their original purpose but instead, have retained their full savage heritage of kill-or-be-killed.

Weaponry can be divided into a number of different categories, including single or double, long or short, rigid or flexible, combinations such as long and short together, and projectile weapons such as the bow and arrow and the blowgun. Most fighting arts of the Philippines begin with the use of sticks and progress to knives and swords. By starting students with weapons, these arts become immediately deadly, which is highly valuable in a society where danger constantly lurks. In such an environment, empty hands are considered a less practical method of fighting, so training evolves toward the most effective application of force: using tools to get the job done.

In the meantime, valuable lessons are learned about footwork and ranging as well as hand/eye, hand/hand, and hand/foot coordination and timing. Patterns originally learned for stick and blade become the tactics for unarmed combat as well. This approach both simplifies and solidifies one's skills for practical self-defense. A final benefit is that the practitioner, having faced weapons everyday in training, develops the confidence and know-how to face weapons in real life, should the need ever occur. Overcoming one's fear can make a crucial difference when one's life is on the line!

In the old days, sticks were used to safely teach basics before students went to "live" steel. Possession of blades, however, was suppressed during the Spanish colonial period, particularly in the northern and central regions. Rattan, a cheap and plentiful vine became the preferred material for training, with hardwoods such as kamagung or bahi used for combat.

Nowadays most arts focus on the use of sticks, which some prefer over blades because of their bone-shattering qualities. Lengths vary from eighteen to thirty-two inches, depending on the characteristics of the system. Some styles involve the measuring of the stick in proportion to the practitioner's body size, such as the length of one's arm, though twenty-eight inches is a standard size. Although the double stick is exciting to watch, with its intricate twirling patterns, the single stick is considered by most masters to be the "heart of the art" because it best teaches the tactical applications of techniques.

A somewhat unique and defining characteristic of the modern FMA is the practice of using numbering systems to teach angles of attack and basing all defenses on understanding the principles of these angles. Whereas most martial arts might teach one technique for a punch, another for a sword, and a third for a kick, in the FMA these will be treated essentially the same if all three strikes are thrown along the same angle. This allows a fast pragmatic integration of training for a wide variety of combat scenarios, including stick, sword, knife, or empty hands.

Many systems use twelve angles of attack, though styles that use more or fewer can also be found. The purpose of learning angles is to recognize incoming attacks so that the mind remains calm while the reflexes take over. A moment's hesitation can be fatal, so training strives towards cultivating instinct rather than intellect. Through this methodology, a good student can become combat proficient in a matter of months instead of years!

Training generally goes through several progressive stages. First comes the learning of the basic techniques for each angle. Almost from the start these will be practiced with a partner to develop a "live" feel by conditioning the reflexes and timing. These techniques will then be incorporated into continuous movement drills. One such drill consists of a partner feeding a pattern of basic attacks while the other counters with defensive techniques. As skill progresses, this can be quite fast-paced and challenging. Another type of drill is "counter for counter," in which one player defends an attack and then counterattacks, thereby feeding a strike for his partner to defend, and so forth. This drill can be as simple as both players feeding the same strike and practicing the same defense repeatedly or it can be as complex as free sparring which uses the full arsenal of techniques in the system.

The Filipino arts often use geometric figures to teach and create techniques. For example, one should understand the combative application of shapes such as squares, triangles, circles, figure eights, and Xs. The square can represent the target zone of your body. Footwork is often based on triangles, either male (focused straight forward) or female (stepping off-line from an incoming attack). Circles can either be patterns of hand/weapon movement or be representative of the safety zone around one's body. A figure eight is a circle inverted upon itself, creating an endless pattern of motion with blade or stick. X visually represents the four most common slashes found within the patterns of the combined downward and upward figure-eight twirls, plus a stab to the center where the lines cross. This is known as *cinco teros,* and represents the first five angles of attack within many systems.

While various styles use different numbering systems, in virtually all of them angle #1 is the right-handed downward forehand slash, striking high to the left side of the head, neck, or collarbone. This is by far the most common blow delivered by humans wielding weapons. The next most common attack is angle #2, the reverse-angle high backhand to the same target areas on the right side of the opponent's body. Together these can be linked to create a figure eight of continuous downward strikes. For every angle there are a handful of simple defensive techniques, but they cover all basic options for countering each attack. Techniques used against one angle may overlap effectively against other angles as well. This quickly builds versatility into the system. Later, variations are developed for each move, until the fighter is able to let reflexes take over. The highest goal is to be able to flow with an opponent, reacting instinctively at any speed.

This concept of flowing movement is embodied in a concept called sinawalli, meaning "weaving." Although commonly thought of as patterns for using double weapons, such as two sticks, sinawalli really refers to any method of intricately coordinating the hands and can be used for double-long weapons, a single stick with check hand, or *espada y daga,* which is the use of a stick or sword in one hand combined with a knife in the other. Through extensive and integrated use of the off (nonprimary-weapon) hand, the Filipino arts are known for skills in checking and trapping an opponent's arms, as well as disarmaments and joint locks.

The off hand is known variously as the check hand, for checking the opponent; the live hand, for its "live" action; or the sacrifice hand, termed so because you sacrifice it to save your life. In the old days the Chinese referred to certain methods of checking with an open thumb as "Filipino hand." Timing in FMA tactics is often a three-count consisting of parry/check/strike. The use of the intermediate check in this sequence is disruptive of an opponent's timing and balance, controlling him to a significantly greater degree than the block/strike combinations found in many empty-hand arts, and highly effective in setting up the finishing blow. The check hand accounts for the high degree of touch sensitivity developed in the training, which allows a fighter to reflexively control or redirect the energy of an opponent.

Styles from the Visayan region of the central Philippines are most often associated with these checking skills. Northern systems use the live hand to a lesser degree, basing their skills more on longer range stick-whipping tactics. Southern Filipinos from the Moslem regions of Mindanao and Sulu are mostly associated with the use of sword or knife, having used their deadly blade

work to preserve much of their independence and culture throughout the 334 years of Spanish occupation.

Part 3: Modern Times

Traffic. It's different in the Philippines. An American wouldn't
have a chance here. Drive down the street on the wrong side; it's
OK, and you can do it at night without headlights. Want to run
a red light? As long as you can squeeze through, feel free to try.

It's no wonder that the martial arts of this country are so good.
The whole culture is geared towards keen reflexes and awareness.
The flow here is not just a martial art concept, it's a pervasive
energy that one experiences continuously in daily life. Filipinos
don't rush like Americans. It is not the speed at which things are
done but the intricacy with which they are interwoven that marks
the character of the islands. Walking, driving, fighting, or just
hanging out, Filipinos are always engaged in a dance with life.

In 1989 I had the good fortune to visit the Philippines as a
member of the first U.S.A. National Escrima team. This affiliation
provided both a buffer against some of the more tiresome aspects
of travel and a connection to the resident martial arts community. It is always more interesting to visit a place when the motivation for going there runs deeper than merely being a tourist.
The First World Full-Contact Escrima/Kali/Arnis Championships
in Cebu, Philippines, provided just the kind of event to bring
together a unique gathering of people with a deep common
interest.

With delegations in attendance from eleven different countries, this was the gala debut of the Filipino martial arts upon the
stage of late twentieth century international martial arts frater-
nization. While the fighting arts of other Asian cultures have had
their day in the sun, bursting into world consciousness and then
blossoming through international organizations and media

coverage, the Filipino arts have always been The Next Big Thing. The arts of Japan came first, then those of Korea—both blessed with large numbers of American troops stationed on their soil throughout the Cold War era and both imbued with strong cultural and organizational skills. They were supported, in some cases, by governmental sponsorship keen on the idea of commercialized cultural exports.

Bruce Lee's explosion into the public eye in the early 1970s provided the fuel to introduce the myriad of martial arts from China, Asia's dominant culture. On his coattails came exposure for lesser known arts that appeared in his films, such as muay thai from Thailand, which flourished especially in Europe because of its spectacular success in the ring. The Filipino arts, however, proved less accessible. Geared for combat, practiced in secrecy, hidden in remote and inhospitable venues, the arts of escrima, kali, arnis, and many others, their names in tongue-twisting local dialects, remained shrouded by myth and misconception. This was about to change, but the process would need nurturing.

In the United States, the groundwork was being laid by a handful of men. The change started slowly, in the small central California city of Stockton, an agricultural center in the San Joaquin Valley. This was home to the largest community of Filipinos in the United States for most of the early twentieth century, many of them farmworkers and laborers who drew together here in "Little Manila" for mutual support and sustenance. Stockton is a hot, dusty town, the kind of place where a dollar is hard earned. Although Filipinos have been a part of American history for centuries, as sailors plying the Manila trade on Spanish galleons, as pirates in the Caribbean, and even as the heroic crew for the pirate Jean Laffite in the Battle of New Orleans against the British in 1814, theirs has been a largely unrecognized contribution.

After serving in World War II alongside U.S. soldiers, many Filipino men settled into life working the fields and orchards of

California and in the fisheries up and down the Pacific coast. While Filipino communities sprang up everywhere, none was larger than Stockton's. It was here that the rebirth of Filipino martial arts flourished.

Among those responsible for this phenomenon, one name stands at the head of the class—that of Angel Cabales, known as the father of escrima in America. In some ways, his is a story similar to many of his generation. Born in 1917 on the Visayan island of Panay, he left the country of his birth in his early twenties to become an itinerant seaman, cannery worker, farm laborer, and finally a farm labor contractor. What separated him from his compatriots were his exceptional skill in stick and knife fighting, and his strong will and fiery temperament.

At the age of thirteen, Angel was befriended by Felicissimo Dizon, arguably the greatest fighter in the Philippines in the twentieth century. Angel became both friend and disciple, learning from Dizon the short-stick art of DeCuerdas escrima. They worked, lived, and trained together in the rough waterfront districts of Manila, earning a reputation as the Escrimador Gang.

As Angel's own reputation grew, he became a bodyguard and then a special policeman, helping clean up trouble spots in this tough and violent environment. Making a name for oneself as a fighter soon led to challenges, and Angel had his share of death matches. Sometimes prearranged, sometimes the result of spontaneous meetings, these death matches did not necessarily result in fatality. Many bouts ended with serious injury to or surrender by the loser, but with whirling sticks or thrusting blades, the threat of death was ever present. Smart and fast, Angel always emerged the victor and from these encounters added to his skill and knowledge. None of his matches ever lasted more than a few seconds.

In 1939 he signed onto a freighter, leaving behind his homeland for ports from the Indian Ocean to the Pacific. By 1941, he left the freighter to stay along the west coast of North America, from

Alaska to Mexico, where he would build his reputation as a fearless and undefeated fighter until his natural death fifty years later.

By the early 1960s, Angel had settled down in Stockton to raise a family. Here he was approached and asked to open an academy for teaching the fighting arts of his homeland, and in 1966, with the help of his business partner Max Sarmiento, Angel opened the first commercial Filipino martial arts academy in the United States. What distinguished his escrima academy was not just the curriculum, which was quite different from that of the karate, tae kwon do and judo available elsewhere, but the fact that, breaking with cultural tradition, Angel opened his school to students of all races. For the first time, Filipino martial arts were being taught to "outsiders." This was a radical departure from the unwritten code that this knowledge was to be shared only with family members or other Filipinos.

In much the same way that Bruce Lee challenged the traditional framework of the Chinese martial arts community and had to fight for the right to teach whomever he chose, Angel Cabales came under fire from other Filipino martial artists who felt similarly betrayed by the prospect of outsiders learning their survival secrets. On several occasions he was challenged to fight; as in the Philippines, he quickly sent his opponents packing.

As word of his academy spread, students from throughout the San Joaquin Valley began to make the trip to train there. Angel soon realized that the harshly realistic training methods from the Philippines would not work as well in this new culture. So he reorganized the art he knew into a more structured teaching format and expanded the training with empty hands to complement the use of weapons. He then renamed his style *serrada,* meaning "closed," to denote the tight characteristics that made it so effective for close-quarter fighting.

Once the door was open, other masters began to follow suit. They quickly realized that not only was such exposure *not* a threat to their survival, but that it also provided a new means of earning a living through their hard-won skills. Still, for many years word about schools for Filipino martial arts was hard to come by, and most students continued to be young Filipinos.

While the first generation masters laid the groundwork for preserving the Filipino martial arts in America, it was one man, Dan Inosanto, who more than anyone else helped propagate the worldwide growth of these arts. Dan, who was living in Los Angeles, had earned a black belt in kenpo under the late grandmaster Ed Parker. Ed had introduced him to the then unknown Bruce Lee. He had also urged Dan to go back to his hometown roots in Stockton to discover the arts that were his heritage, and thus began a lifelong quest to seek out and bring forth the knowledge of the old masters.

Dan grew to prominence through his role as training partner for Bruce Lee, in addition to a film career of his own that began with a famous stick and nunchuk duel with Bruce in *Game of Death*. After Bruce died, many fans in the martial arts looked to Dan to continue Bruce's fledgling system of jeet kune do. Jeet kune do is actually a concept for learning rather than a fighting system, so Dan turned to the Filipino arts as the best model for demonstrating the concepts of jeet kune do in action. In addition, Dan published *The Filipino Martial Arts* (Know Now Publishing, 1980) a book that became the bible of the subject. Through this work, people worldwide became aware of these beautiful, deadly arts and the men who were teaching them. Students began to flock to Dan's school in southern California, and through seminars and teacher certification programs, Dan reached out to communities around the globe, helping plant seeds of this art in places where it had never grown before.

As awareness of FMA grew throughout the 1980s, coverage began to increase in the martial arts magazines. This created for the first time a wider exposure for many of the other masters. One began to hear of established teachers from the East Coast, such as Professor Visitation, creator of *v-arnis jitsu*; Amante P. Marinas, teaching *pananandata*; and Leo Gaje, inheritor of his family's *pekiti tirsia* system. On the West Coast, belated recognition brought some of the old masters their moment of glory, even bringing a few back from retirement to pass along and preserve their art.

By the mid-1980s, Filipino martial arts were entering a new phase. A new generation of instructors began to spread the art, and interest began to grow in Europe, particularly in Germany and England. Dan Inosanto conducted seminars abroad, and his students, such as Paul Vunak and Cass Magda, began to make names for themselves through their teaching. Another student, Graciella Casillas, became famous as the only person to ever hold simultaneous world championships in both boxing and kickboxing. From Angel's serrada system came Jimmy Tacosa, Mike Inay, and Rene Latosa, the latter two of whom created their own separate styles from their common roots in Angel's system, and who eventually became better known in Germany than in their own California hometowns.

The increased level of activity in the Filipino martial arts community did not go unnoticed back in the Philippines. The masters there recognized the lucrative potential in the overseas market and began to reach out. Among them were Ernesto Presas, younger brother of Remy; Edgar Sulite, of Lameco escrima; and Dionisio Canete, a master with Doce Pares in Cebu. Many of these men became jet-age teachers, flying between the Philippines, the United States, and Europe. More dedicated students began to make the trek back to the home bases in the Philippines, seeking out the older masters still living there, such as Eulogio and Cacoy Canete, Tatang Ilustrissimo, Jose Mena, Benjamin Luna Lema, and others.

The most active organization to build a worldwide base was Doce Pares, based in the Philippines in Cebu. Dionisio Canete, a lawyer with political ambitions, channeled his considerable energies into developing an organization in the United States, beginning with Alfredo Bandalan's club in San Jose, California. As point man for this association, Alfredo organized the first U.S. National Championship tournament in San Jose in 1988 under the banner of NARAPHIL-USA, an affiliate of the national governing board in the Philippines.

This event was the precursor to the creation of the U.S. National Escrima Team, which in 1989 would go to the Philippines as the official delegation to the organizing congress for the World Eskrima/Kali/Arnis Federation (WEKAF). This congress, held in Cebu just prior to the first World Championships, was attended by most of the prominent masters and grandmasters in the Philippines, who comprised the board of the government-sponsored martial arts organization NARAPHIL. The authority invested in this body for organizing and promoting the indigenous martial arts of the Philippines was rolled over into the new organization, WEKAF, to promote the Filipino arts and competitions on a worldwide basis. The WEKAF congress, which was duly chartered on August 1989, ended with a pre-tournament motorcade that paraded through Cebu City, bringing forth the enthusiasm of the local populace and raising excitement to a level usually reserved in the United States for major sporting events. Attendance at the tournament would at times overflow from the seats onto the floor as Filipinos celebrated the homecoming of their art.

Part 4: The Crystal Ball

What's next for the Filipino martial arts? For years there has been an expectation that the FMA will be The Next Big Thing to hit the martial arts. There have been many trends since the 1950s: judo, karate, tae kwon do, kung fu, jeet kune do, injutsu, muay thai, kickboxing, aikido, Brazilian jiujitsu, etc. One thing seems certain: that in our fad-driven, short-attention-span, high-speed world at the end of the twentieth century, fads come and go faster all the time. On the other hand, a fighting art with the characteristics of the Filipino systems—fast moving, quickly decisive, easily learned—should fit into this lifestyle. Perhaps, though, it helps to turn the perspective around and look at where the art is now, and how far it has come.

Only thirty years ago, the Filipino martial arts were dying, the skills held tightly by a handful of old men and passed down to one or two family members in living rooms, if it was taught at all. Since then, the FMA have grown into an internationally recognized method of self-defense, with tens of thousands of practitioners worldwide in hundreds of schools and clubs.

Full-contact competition is held in over a dozen countries, leading to national championships and placement in international competition. The goal, as envisioned by WEKAF founder Dionisio Canete, is eventually to make it into the Olympics. The Classic Eskrima Championships, devised by Ronald A. Harris, represent yet another highly ambitious format. Several tournaments, held in San Diego in 1992, 1993, and 1994, introduced cultural and fighting aspects neglected in other competitions. In addition to martial art forms, traditional music and dance were also featured. Unique to these tournaments were fighting divisions not only for single stick but also double stick and *espada y daga*. Fighters were limited to minimal padding, which included helmets and light gloves, plus elbow, knee, and groin protection. Unlike the competitions in WEKAF, no padded jackets were used. Punching, kicking, takedowns, and submission grappling were allowed in the single- and double-stick formats, helping raise the level of realistic contact.

Still others pursue the limits of friendly full-contact experience outside of the ring, most notably the Dog Brothers Incorporated Martial Arts, founded by Marc "Crafty Dog" Denny. The Dog Brothers host "real contact stick fighting" in parks, where participants are limited to the use of fencing, helmets, and light gloves for protection. This increases realism, and prevents the slugfests often engaged in by heavily padded fighters in formal tournament fighting. The Dog Brothers' motto is "Higher consciousness through harder contact!"

The variety of what can be found within the framework of these arts is limited only by imagination. The truth of the matter is that FMA are not arts that will ever appeal to the general public. They just look too intimidating for the average person to imagine doing themselves. As an instructor in serrada since 1986, I've seen big, tough full-contact fighters come to watch a class and walk away muttering about how crazy we are. Ironically, these arts are actually safer and less painful to learn than most empty-handed systems. Unlike those martial arts, where students regularly punch each other and bang together arms and legs, the FMA are generally taught stick-to-stick for safety. Sticks feel no pain, so there is relatively little need for body conditioning to learn the art. At most, one will occasionally get a knuckle popped, though training does carry the caveat of practicing carefully. Of course, advanced sessions get much faster and more aggressive, but by then practitioners should know what to do, and safety gear such as helmets and gloves are sometimes used when testing the limits of control.

The percentage of students within the martial arts who will dedicate themselves to the Filipino arts will probably remain small. In spite of its growth, the arts of escrima/kali/arnis will always be strong drink, not to everybody's taste. As we end the second millennium, the savage fighting arts of seafaring pirates have come to find acceptance, and even respectability, in our modern age. The magnificent and efficient fighting arts of the South Seas have finally been let out of the proverbial bag to take their place on the world stage among the great fighting disciplines of other cultures and to shine as a true gift of knowledge from the Filipino people.

Jôgo De Capoeira: In Motion

Bira Almeida

The career of the *capoeirista* begins with the *batisado*. From their first *jôgo* to the point of fully understanding the art, students will spend many years constantly training and probing their weaknesses, facing the treacheries of life with open eyes. During this time, they will evolve through various stages of development that inevitably will be physical, mental and spiritual as they strive toward a well-rounded study of the art. An isolated focus on any one of those aspects will bring limited results and breed imperfect *capoeiristas*.

The journey through the stages of development will be continuous with no abrupt advances along the way. Students cannot jump from one plateau to the next but must climb slowly and carefully, following a natural process that comes from dedicated training and a feeling of well-being in the art. It never should be a hasty and neurotic attempt to progress prematurely, or a plunge into unhealthy and excessive work toward unattainable goals. *Capoeiristas,* however, must fully commit themselves in every *jôgo,* continuously striving to play beyond falsely perceived points that we may believe to be our limits. Seemingly, limitations of knowledge, age, or even experience over opponents should not cause *capoeiristas* to give up striving toward their full potential; nor should the amount of toil, occasional pains, or previous failure discourage anyone from starting anew each *jôgo*. The goals one sets in capoeira define the categories of *discípulo, contra-mestre* and *mestre*. The majority of *capoeiristas* are *discípulos* who live the art as a complementary activity to the other activities in their life. They are satisfied simply to have capoeira in their hearts and to improve the quality of their lives through its practice.

Contra-mestres are *capoeiras* who definitely have reached the maximum of their physical potential, who dedicate time to internalize the philosophy of capoeira, and who have a strong desire to pass on the tradition of the art.

Mestres are those who have crossed the paths of *discípulo* and *contra-mestre,* who totally open their selves to an understanding of the spiritual dimension of the art, and who are totally committed to devote a lifetime helping others discover, enjoy and become initiated into capoeira.

On the first level, students begin to learn clear and defined movements of attack and defense, developing discipline and self-control. They jump into the *jôgo* without knowing exactly what is happening. They are lost in space; they see nothing. Not only do the movements of the opponents seem to materialize by magic, but their own movements are beyond control. I call this stage "playing in the dark."

Capoeiristas progressively gain a clear perception of their own movements as they begin to apply different variations for kicking and body positioning according to their personalities and the needs of the *jôgo*. They become aware of the blows that could have taken their heads off, and can feel the defense against their most effective attacks. Although seeing the game, students at this level do not yet have sufficient experience and physical skill to use the capoeira movements properly. I call this stage "playing in the water" because the lack of knowledge and skill at this level constricts the possibility of constant flow and consistent effective action.

In the next stage, "playing in the light," students work to perfect their movements, the timing and rhythm of their fighting. As the sharpness of their game improves and their bodies learn to respond correctly to the tactics of the *jôgo,* they become able to defend and attack with precision, power and grace. They are now mature fighters who demonstrate impeccable skill in using proper capoeira techniques, and who know how to transform the *jôgo* with completely new and unexpected movements in the heat of the battle. At this point, the emphasis in training must change from physical achievements to controlling of emotions and comprehension of philosophy. This is the level one must reach in order to become a *contra-mestre.*

I reached the stage of "playing in the light" many years training so intensely that I lost eight pounds each session. I was a fighting machine, challenging my own limits, other *capoeiristas* and martial artists of different styles. After years of "playing in the light," I thought I had such good physical skills and strong attitude that I had no longer any challenging opponent. I had supposedly reached my limits, and from there had sunk into a depression with no motivation to train for what I thought to be just a slight possibility of physical and technical improvement. I was stuck in front of a large stone wall created by my own limited perceptions, which did not let me see anything more in capoeira. So I went to business school and decided to outfit myself in a suit. I graduated four years later, got married, moved to Sao Paulo and worked for a big company. I was still teaching capoeira but training very little outside classes. When I returned to Bahia, I spent three years without training, teaching, or even hearing a *berimbau.*

I assumed I was finished with capoeira. I got fat and complacent. Then, one inspiring day, I faced myself again. A strong and fresh breeze was blowing me out of darkness and once more I began training. At the end of the first day, with an entire leg bruised and with excruciating pain, I smiled. For the first time in my life I saw the art from this side and understood how presumptuous I had been. I had thought I knew everything about capoeira. Such foolishness! Even physically I still had a lot to experience. I held back my vanity and decided to rejoin the road a thousand miles behind the point where I had left off. It was difficult to start again but I had a new challenge, a strong and valid enemy to motivate myself, my own weakness. A few years later I felt physically comfortable again and traced my steps back to the stone wall which had blocked my way in the past. I found it not so impenetrable. The wall represented the border between the physical and spiritual aspects of capoeira. Studying capoeira philosophy, I envisioned a path through this wall and began to discover a new dimension to the art. I felt much closer to the old *mestres* whom I had known. Many of them were no longer playing capoeira, but they carried a very special quality, like a brilliant flame reflecting something beyond themselves. I was not able to understand the importance of this quality before. Now it touched me like a beam from a distant lighthouse, guiding my steps. It was the awareness of where I had been, and where I could go along the capoeira path. To achieve this quality, to accept who I was, to know who I wanted to be, to know who I really could be, seemed far away, but I decided to go ahead in the belief that one day it would come to me. Then I felt my feet treading strongly on the path.

My progress in capoeira has been following the lines of a spiral divided into three sections representing "playing in the dark," "playing in the water," and "playing in the light." After some time of dynamic improvement in the level of "playing in the light" I reached another frontier where a new perspective opened up and I started to learn again as a beginner—"playing in the dark." Many times after reaching the level of "playing in the light," dealing with a tiresome and challenging situation, I wanted to remain there forever, stagnating my search for knowledge. This complacent attitude bound me to a particular level of understanding that I only overcame when I surpassed my fears of accepting a new and valid challenge. I think that in order to progress in capoeira as well as in life one must have a curiosity and drive for more knowledge, even when the sacrifice of the comfort of "playing in the light" of already known stages.

My current perception of the *jôgo* itself has been of inestimable value in playing successfully with my students. One may say that they are beginners not ready to confront experienced *capoeiristas*. Many of them, however, have solid backgrounds in other martial arts and are strong fighters; yet, most of the time, their skills are not a real obstacle to my control of the *jôgo*. This may confirm the validity of the subtle sense of timing and economy of movements as positive acquisitions that older *capoeiras* can rely on. I think that I am beginning to perceive the spiritual body of power of real mastery that transcends age or physical prowess. This concept is very much a result of my aging as an active *capoeirista* as well as my North American experience. Bringing capoeira to a culture in which it manifests differently has been broadening my perception.

To expose my students to a more diversified and Brazilian approach and to expand their knowledge through training with other *mestres,* I have promoted workshops including other experts of the art. When Camisa came to the United States we had the chance to play a lot. It was a difficult experience for me after five years without facing a technically solid *capoeirista*. After the first day of workshop, we went to the Mission Cultural Center studio and played and discussed capoeira until four in the morning. This interaction clarified some of the concepts I had developed far from the capoeira mainstream. Being away from Brazil for so long undoubtedly had allowed me to take different perspectives on the art and to see and to understand things that I could not have seen or understood had I remained there. My ideas generated in such a removed context, however, had to face the native reality of capoeira to take on real substance in the *jôgo* to affirm or contest their validity. My re-encounter with Camisa brought this home to me.

It is said in martial arts that the ones who stay true may become wise masters, possessing such a spirit and knowledge that they are able to defeat the younger, even if they are physically stronger. Perhaps this is true, despite the obviously large number of contrived situations where young students help the old master to perform well, respectfully holding back real attacks. In capoeira, this is more difficult because, beside technical knowledge and endurance, the *jôgo* also demands flexibility and quick reflexes, physical qualities that are dulled during the aging process. So, an old active *capoeirista* generally will not be that successful against the younger ones, unless he had developed special qualities to compensate for the decrease in physical capabilities.

Some time ago, I was able to achieve a level in which my physical qualities and technical knowledge became merely a step to another dimension of capoeira that I called "playing with the crystal ball." At this level, I have been attempting "to read" the opponent's mind, conducting the *jôgo* by setting myself in the right place at the right time. My journey along this path has been a very difficult and painful process of growth, involving self-control, patience and the capacity of exercising a positive resistance against the odds, not only in the *roda* but in my personal life. Sometimes it seems to me that it has taken too many years of physical training, too much emotional struggle in confronting my feelings and values, and an apparently irrational and unnerving effort to open myself to spiritual insights beyond my understanding.

Recently, I have been thinking about another level in capoeira as an ultimate stage that one may possibly attain as a reward for so much struggling, "playing with the mind." Stories about capoeira and famous *capoeiristas* of the past allude to skills, knowledge and power beyond normal comprehension. There were *capoeiras* with *corpo fechado* (closed bodies), invulnerable to bullets; *capoeiras* who transformed themselves into animals or trees to escape persecution; *capoeiras* who disappeared at will in a moment of necessity, fighters undefeated in impossible situations; and healers of extraordinary success. There are no rational explanations for the feats of many in the lore of the art.

Sometimes, during rare *jôgos,* situations arise that cannot be explained through physical and technical resources, such as when a *capoeirista* seems to have absolute control of the opponent's will. In the level of "playing with the mind," I envision that the opponents do what you are almost silently ordering them to do. It is not only the advantage of experience or technical knowledge, but a special force, an *aché,* which undoubtedly must have no purpose other than to help one's opponent evolve and reach a universal harmony through the capoeira way. To me this must be a quality of *mestres* who care only about the development of their students, and not about themselves any longer.

From the beginning to their graduation, students must walk far enough and long enough to pass through the physical stages of "playing in the dark," "playing in the water," and "playing in the light." From this point on they must free their minds and bodies from tensions and techniques, and open the door for spontaneous movements. They must learn to play capoeira from the inside out, with their hearts: the way of *contra-mestres.* After that, the feet of *capoeiristas* will be tired and sore from the rocks on the path, but their spirits will help them to "play with the crystal ball," mastering timing, economy of movement and attuning themselves to the universal rhythm of life. If they continue studying the art and exploring the absolute boundaries of their physical limits, and if they have the courage and humility to accept the beginner's challenge of playing in the dark of new situations, they may become able to "play with the mind," a quality of *mestres* touched by the blessing of the *orixás*.

Terry Dobson
Yawns in Slumber

Riki Moss

while you and I have lips and voices
which are for kissing and to sing with
who cares if some one-eyed son of a bitch
invents a machine to measure spring with ...

e.e. cummings

In a dark log cabin at the edge of a northern lake, a fifty-three year old martial artist in his bright new underwear sat down in front of a monumental butcher-block tabletop which rested on two marble legs the shape of winged bulls. A colorful dust: terra cotta from the dissolving logs, the blackish powders of demolition, white talc of decomposition, green of immobilized slime, coated everything. What light penetrated the filthy skylights hugged the backs of dust particles falling at random around the neglected room. Small creatures lived in the dresser drawers. From the enormous paw print embedded in dried mud on the faded oriental carpet, it appeared that some massive cat had wintered over.

As far as I'm concerned I have a problem and I would be grateful for any assistance to get me through it.

He wore an old navy-blue sweater, marine issue, the kind with elbow patches and itchy looking lint over a black tee shirt. He leaned back in his chair with one bare leg up on the table and the other stretched out in front of him. Fleecy socks covered his feet. He was dressed for writing. He was ready, except he couldn't think of anything real to say. The problem was, he hadn't been doing physical aikido for years. The problem was, in the deplorable shape he was in, he was ashamed to roll. He saw himself on his back, tears in his eyes, legs flailing. And how could you write about aikido if you couldn't roll? The problem was, without being on the mat, he had no right opening his mouth. He put his hands in front of him with the fingers touching; his mouth was about to open for nothing—an enormous sin, in his opinion, right up there with greed and lack of compassion.

If he were still on his feet, if he still was an aikidoist, he would be covering up his discomfort by leading a class in a little meditative walking. *Let us now do* tenkan. And hopefully something coherent would occur to him before they got to the far wall.

Let us now do tenkan *across the room. Good. Here's what* tenkan *did for me at the House of Dior. It was really funny. I had a plane ticket and $20.00 to get back to Tokyo. I had to stop in Okinawa and Hong Kong. I had one suit. At some point on the plane, I split the seam in my pants. I didn't have any thread so I couldn't sew them up. I just had to get to the Dior collection. I knew that if I went back to Tokyo with a program and said, "Oh, by the way, I just went to the Dior collection," that would get me the job I wanted as a spy in the world of fashion. With my butt hanging out, I went to Dior. All the salesgirls are at least a countess or above, right? It's just the most elegant place. It's the last place in the world you go with your crotch ripped out of your pants. "Where's the collection?" I asked. And they said, "Up there." 'There' is a magnificent French staircase with all these people, the Duke* *de so and so, the queen mother, whatever, going up there with little poodles. I have to climb that staircase. So, what can I do? I do tenkan, very slow butt squeezing tenkans up those steps. I looked at the ceiling and I kept moving. Now, do* tenkan *as if your life depended on it.*

Once he had something, he would spin around. Moving shockingly fast for the old, decrepit bear he was, he would reverse his steps without warning. Then he'd shout, Bow to the person next to you. Deal with whomever God has sent you to work with! And then for a few moments, as he scanned his own mind for the subject God had (God willing) sent him to teach, his students fell all over themselves trying to achieve their versions of a world class bow.

But he had not been on his feet for some time. Since his last surgery, the one in which his lungs were scraped clean with increasingly tiny tools, he found it embarrassing to roll. Despite their thickness, his thighs were fragile with disuse. His purple ankles were swollen. Long scars from previous caresses with surgical implements cupped his knees. A brutal infection ran down his left shinbone like a swollen lip. It had been many years since he last shouted into the expectant face of a student or experienced the excitement of igniting a deserving mind. The martial artist was confined to his language from now on.

I want to take something that I did with O-Sensei* and transform this into American language. But I have this problem. I'm a Gemini, I have two sides. One side is O'Sensei's student, the messenger of peace, non-violence and all that. The other side is the kind that will go and work in a bar.

So, this was Terry Dobson. A man who took some credit for bringing the Japanese art of aikido to the United States. An author as well as aikido teacher. The black beret on his head was the same

---

* O-Sensei is the formal form of address for Morihei Ueshiba (1883–1969), the founder of aikido. Terry Dobson was the only American student whom Ueshiba accepted as one of his personal students.

one he sported fifteen years ago when his last book was published. This was not a writer's affectation; it was just his hat. What you see is what you get. His appearance advertised someone who has seen conflict and not always from the right side. And yet, underlying the grime lay elegance. His bearing suggested more than a hint of grace. This could be a man of erudition, someone to the manor born.

Slumped in his chair, considering his problem, Terry tried on a look that said, loudly and unequivocally, "Bouncer." His upper lip curled in a right-sided snarl. His eyes narrowed. His neck retreated into his shoulders; his chest inflated, even his feet got bigger. He did this well. He could rile himself up and become truly formidable. There *was* an actual deep evil inside him which, when allowed to look through his eyes, regarded the world without appetite or longing or regret.

So later, at the football game, when I knocked that kid's teeth out, when people were congratulating me and when I really wasn't sorry, I knew they were applauding some being inside me who was totally evil. And the implications of that were frightening.

Unlike Terry's imagined hero, personally, he hated bars. His mother's alcoholism turned him off the booze vibe and besides, you couldn't smoke dope in bars. But it seemed to him that if you wanted to know whether aikido worked off the mat—and it was a question which every aikidoist ought to ask himself—a tavern was an appropriate testing ground: let's see if you could avoid punching out someone's lights when you really did have a knife at your throat. So in 1972, he got himself a job as a bouncer in a Burlington bar.

I had to stand in the doorway. Now this is a very honored position, that of the seneschal who determines who gets in and who doesn't, the major duomo who says "Her Royal Highness, the Princess of Sweden." The place itself seemed mythic, like a gloomy medieval hall. I was the doorkeeper deciding which peasants could get to come in to get drunk and fall down in the sawdust. Most of these peasants were really nice college kids, reasonably educated and well mannered. I had fun with them. But as time wore on I started losing my perspective. Some fourteen year old would whine, "Don't I look eighteen?" And I'd say, "You're too fucking stupid to have an age."

One night I went to work early. There is hardly anybody in the place. The bartender, a little tiny guy, Sam Fish, is back there doing his bar number, bringing out his beers, and I say, "What's up, Sam?" He says, "How're ya doing?" I say, "What's shakin'?" He says, "You see that guy over there?"

I look and I see what seems like a pile of leather coats but is actually a guy. He's huge, the biggest goddamn thing I've ever seen in my life. I say to Sam, "So what's with him?"

Sam says, "I don't know. He was drunk when I got here. I got busy, and he went to sleep. You gotta wake him up and get him out of here."

I go over. I poke through the leather. "Sir? Excuse me, sir? Hey, sir, you can't sleep here, this is not a fucking train station." After a few minutes, the mound starts stirring. He rises up, blinking his eyes. I hand him a cup of coffee and turn away, but then: bam! It is definitely trouble. I spin around. There's a kid on the floor in front of the men's room door. The big guy had opened the door to go in there and slammed it up against this kid who had been standing in the corner. He served him up just like a tennis ball, knocked him ass over tea kettle about ten yards away.

The kid jumps up and says, "Hey, asshole!" and he walks right back to the exact spot where he had been standing. Talk about tactics. Doug, that's the drunk's name, goes for it again. He opens the door and for the second time knocks the kid on the floor. By this time, I'm over there. I see that this is a nerdy kid and this is Doug, right? So I say to Doug, "Doug, don't sweat the nerdy kids. Believe me, they are not even worth your time." He says, "I just wanna go to the men's room."

I say, "So go to the men's room."

"You mean to tell me I can't go to the men's room?" he says.

169

"Wha?" I say.

"You mean to tell me I can come in this bar, spend my money and you won't let me go into the bathroom to piss it out?"

"No, no, please go to the men's room," I say to him. "Feel welcome to use the facilities. As a matter of fact, I will stand outside and make sure nobody else comes in so that you can have the men's room to yourself." Now, it seemed to me that we were both on the same side. I'm doing aikido. This could work. He wants to go to the men's room and I was urging him to do so. I tell him, "Consider me your servant in making certain nobody interrupts you."

The trouble was, he didn't think I was on his side. "How dare you," he yelled. "How dare you." What he wants to do is hammer the shit out of me. What I want to do is aikido.

Doug starts sliding his leather jacket down his arms. I think I know exactly what is coming. He's going to flip that thing over my head, his hand is going back either for a punch or for a knife, a gun. And when that hand comes out, with whatever it is he carries on his hip, it's going to be coming fast, and so I am going to have to move before he does. So I slam him through the bathroom. I have my hand on his throat and I can hear his head snap. I have forgotten all about my desire to do aikido. Instead, I am hitting him as hard as I can. Now, Doug is a very big man, a good 6'6" and 300 pounds. And as I stood there whopping him, it seemed to me that he was getting even bigger.

He started getting bigger and bigger, until he seemed to me as big as my father. And as he grew, I could feel the rage I felt for my father grow with him. Everything was happening in slow motion. I could hear the milliseconds ticking slowly away. I had him by the throat; he was my father. I felt my hand move up as if by itself. My fingers shot out, and I stuck them deep into the sockets of his eyes. I stopped just before causing him any real harm. But Doug didn't know that. He screamed. And as he screamed, he let go of his bladder.

He really did have to piss. The force of his piss coming through his underwear and his trousers turned into the most beautiful nimbus. It was

*golden; it was golden mist. The light was coming from behind him. There
was this great shadow. I remember the observer part of me thinking that
it was beautiful. We were in this toilet, where there was just shit and piss
and beer and sawdust, and pink walls with graffiti, swastikas and lines
like "death to faggots." And all of a sudden, it became like a grotto at
Lourdes or something. This piss, it was golden, and it was pervasive.*

*You know that when my teacher, O-Sensei, talked about his enlight-
enment, he said that he felt himself surrounded by a golden mist. And
so here I was with this in my consciousness. I thought, "Oh, that's
funny." I get my own kind of golden mist, and in its own way, it was
as beautiful as his, just as gorgeous. Then it struck me that this was a
kind of enlightenment for me, that my enlightenment could come here
in the toilet. You can't really see light unless it falls in a dark place.*

The cabin Terry sat in was one of seven at the edge of a silty lake
willed to him by his grandparents. Constructed at the turn of the
century out of vertical cedar logs milled from the copse in which
it was meant to nestle, the cabin sat as close to the lake's edge as
the law would allow. When his grandfather first came to this island,
he floated a barge of cement up the Hudson, through the locks and
then north with the current, hugging the Vermont shore. He insisted
it would be an adequate container for the lake when it let go of its
ice in the spring. The natives laughed in his face. They were right;
he was wrong. After the ice retreated, his precious wall was spread
like a bread crumb trail from him to his bullheaded stupidity. The
cabin was at least thirty feet above the high water mark and over
the years it had tilted and buckled. Nothing was level. Each winter the water table scarred a new path through the foundation.
Everything inside built up patinas of rot, mildew or mold.

With his mother and her husband, stepbrothers, brothers, nan-
nies, cooks and gardeners, Terry had been coming here since he
was born. Even with the entourage, the kids were freer here than
in their Park Avenue penthouse. Terry was happy. So, when his

mother, sick and bored, abandoned the place in the 1970s, Terry returned from his ten years in Japan to try and make himself a home. But his timing was off. He wasn't ready yet. For the next fifteen years, he traveled from one coast to another. In 1984, in San Francisco, he found himself in a difficult situation: too many drugs, the beginning signs of serious ill health, too much of everything except love and peace, success, respect and money.

There were too many dakini *coming to my cabin saying, oh, sensei, you have such a big heart. What was I supposed to do? I felt deeply disgusted with myself.*

In sunny California, his dark side was standing out like a contagious disease. The prescription was, seriously, to get out of town.

But where was he going to go? Although he founded a few dojos, was welcomed in many, at least for a time, at least as a guest, he never really had a dojo of his own. And with his equation of aikido with life, not having a dojo was not having a home. Then in 1985 his mother died, leaving her sons fifteen exquisitely neglected acres on Lake Champlain. Terry, suspecting he was seriously ill, gathered his belongings which had been scattered like footprints all over the country, packed up the furniture discarded in his ancestral penthouse, and moved to Vermont.

He unpacked his old Selectric, screwed a typewriter roller to the wall, bought himself a roll of paper and went to work. If you just study O-Sensei, you get a very bland philosophy. Philosophy can easily get into preaching, become a sort of trap for nonviolence. Bending into the keyboard, he started feeling some long overdue energy, he was getting something now. The trouble was that, as far as he was concerned, he had a problem. So far, he had been talking about his life in his own voice. By narrating himself, he wasn't able to comment upon it; he wasn't allowed to play. In 1960 an incident occurred on Mountain spur railway, which wound deep through the Japanese Alps, passing little hamlets of houses clinging to cliffs.

It was Saturday morning; people got on and off the train. There were old people going to market, farmers with their chickens and pigs and a lot of college kids on a mountain climbing vacation. The sun was streaming in through the window. Everybody was happy. The college kids had their gear stuffed up in the baggage rack, mostly rucksacks with ice axes tied to them. They were singing German mountain climbing songs with Japanese accents, which I found greatly amusing. Across from me was this beautiful old bald man dozing in the warm sun. When the train stopped, most of the kids got up to get off. One of them was next to me; he yanked his rucksack off the rack and the ice axe fell like a guillotine right into the beautiful old man's bald head.

I froze. The axe clattered to the floor. The old man woke up and clutched his head. Blood started squirting from the wound. He looked up at the kid who was absolutely aghast. The kid looked about to have a heart attack. The old man saw that the boy had no idea of what to do. He reached down, grabbed the ice axe and handed it to the kid with a bow. He said, "Have a good day. Enjoy your climb." How is that for deep humility. I hope that when I get to be that age and have an ice axe in my head, I'll remember to bow.

Terry looked up and scratched his nose. His glasses, held on with a piece of duct tape, slid halfway down.

I have to give these lines to someone else! That's how to get the juice in this kind of writing, juice, realness, and relevance to our world. There's got to be fiction here! I can't just write Terry Dobson's stories. I mean, who is Terry Dobson? So he studied with the O-Sensei? So what.

He took off his glasses and rubbed his eyes, leaned back in his chair.

What I'm trying to do seems to me like climbing Everest from the inside.

He looked around at his cabin and saw how decrepit it was. As for himself, he felt just like the pieces of deconstructing furniture piled all over the room: a three-legged couch, paisley pillows with the stuffing hanging out, and—there he was, Terry Dobson, author.

He squinted into space and twirled the fringes of the yellowed silk aviator's scarf that hung loosely around his neck. Dust swirled about his shoulders, sending him into a coughing fit. He coughed so spastically that his entire body convulsed. His face looked crushed and grew alarmingly red. He had to hold onto the arms of his chair until the fit passed and he was able to gather his breath.

I can't just go around saying all this bland stuff about myself! I need the Virgil leading Dante and Beatrice to paradise and the inferno, Virgil whose wisdom is from copious knowledge and kindness. Larger than life, larger than me! One who is some sort of apotheosis. That doesn't mean that he isn't dark, and he isn't seamy. He traces the edges, the margins of society. Every once in awhile, for reasons he doesn't understand, he starts drinking or gets into a combat situation. He could pass on every level of society, depending on his clothes. There is a wonderful line by Chandler: "Down these mean streets must walk someone who is not himself mean." Unfortunately, I'm too mean to ever be chief, but I appreciated people who might be looking for those qualities.

There's too much made of enlightenment. What we need is endarkenment.

The afternoon deepened, its light turning golden even as the room itself grew darker. The clumps of horsehair, which had been used to stuff the cracks between the logs and were now fallen about the floor, were transformed by the light into angel's hair. The sunset on the other side of the island was magnificent, its residual aura was this evening especially lavish. It glowed through the narrow skylight under which Terry sat, bathed in a rich, Byzantine light. Around him, the darkness was glowing.

On the wall hung two portraits in matching ornate gold frames of seated men in uniforms. They had similar serious expressions, men made tedious by the weight of their wars. Bathed in the light of their time, they stared from their murky backgrounds, with Terry between them as if parenthetically.

I grew up flanked by two portraits of two warriors, Daniel Boone and my ancestor, also named Daniel. Their mementos, their stuff was all around. They really fed into my warrior trip. One story about Daniel Boone involves aiki. *Captured by indians and tortured in horrible ways, he eventually figured out how to escape. He started telling them, "You guys should stop following me. You should stop looking at me. I don't want to leave, this is a perfect life. Why would anybody want to leave this life?" After a while, they would say, "Oh, all right."*

One day, it was a beautiful warm spring day. They had plenty of meat. Everybody was just hanging out. Boone went around, and he took the lead shot out of the indian's rifles and put them in his pocket. Then he said, "Bye, bye assholes!" And he started running. The indians started shooting. He turned around after he got a couple of hundred yards and made a show of catching the bullets. He then ran back and gave back their bullets, the ones he'd stashed in his pockets.

He said, "You guys are silly. Do you think I'd run away?" They were so amused by that, they stopped following him. Then he split for real. He ran for five days straight. They kept after him, but never caught him. That running back and pretending to catch the bullets, that's *aiki*. That's really deep *aiki*. That's taking their psychological expectations and turning them around.

Well, of course no man can catch bullets. But you can do something, O-Sensei knew that. In Manchuria, it is said that O-Sensei used to do get up on the battlements and chuck moons at the Russians. **He'd drop trou and all sort of unseemly things.** *But the Russians, who were sniping at him, could never hit him. Word got to the Japanese war correspondents, who came to him and said, "We hear you can dodge bullets." He said, "Nobody can dodge bullets. When a man makes up his mind to injure another person, there's a spark. You can see that. If you move at that spark, you can be way ahead of the bullet."*

Terry's eyes moved from his dour ancestor, the propertied winner of the first Purple Heart, to the more infamous Daniel Boone and back again. These men were in his genes and right now, they

175

felt ominous. Terry's deep paranoia, always waiting in the wings, was knocking at the edge of his consciousness.

Who is out there trying to hurt me? Aiki *is a flow of spirit from me to my attacker. I must not separate myself from him. His thoughts must be mine, I can know his intent to move before it happens. My* ki *connects to the earth and is grounded. That's how it happens. There is nothing separating us. Who is out there? What can I do?*

The answer came, loud and clear.

If someone wants to attack you, help him. Don't put up a wall of resistance, but rather, blend your energy with his and help him on his way. Love him when you do this. Make him your brother. No one is going to mess with my brother. He is my flesh and blood, I want only for his well being. At the same time, I don't have to take any shit from my brother. As long as I am sincere in this, we won't fight. It would be senseless. Have you ever seen a boxing match where anyone punches himself? Fighting my brother is fighting myself: I am not going to punch myself. So, make a brother of your enemy. Whomever attacks is already defeated: by attacking, he has already lost. And then, when he's on the floor help him to his feet, thank him and bow. Bow when you come into the dojo, bow when you step onto the mat, bow towards the tokanoma. *That is the place where God dwells, where the soul of the art dwells. Bow, and be on full alert.*

The spirit in which you bow is important. You reveal yourself by the way you bow. An empty bow, while better than no bow, is essentially worthless. As you bend at the waist and at the neck, you'll want to experience a feeling of vulnerability and humility. Your bow makes you an empty vessel into which knowledge can be poured. If you bow well to a partner, even a stranger, that person will immediately be fully conscious of you. The bow is not a quaint custom. Bow to your teacher every time he comes by. You thank him. You thank your partner for any kind of instruction given to you. Should you unconsciously be the cause of injury to another person, bow to them. Should another person cause you injury, bow to him as well. Thank him for the experience. When in doubt, bow.

Terry put his hands around his leg. It felt stiff, foreign to his body, bloodless and wooden as a club. He lifted it off and put it down with a thud next to his other leg. Spreading his knees, reweighting himself on the balls of his feet, he slid off his chair and lowered himself onto one knee. Then he pressed his other knee toward the ground. Eventually, he was down on both knees. Even such simple movements were affecting his breathing. Another coughing spasm gathered in his throat. A cloud passed over the skylight. Terry looked up to watch it slide by. He felt exhausted and hopeless.

I want to transform something that I did with O-Sensei and trans-form this into American language. I'm trying to write about aikido without practicing it. I need to bow! Make me that empty vessel into which knowledge can be poured.

Why had he been foolish enough to think that this telling of his life, this writing of aikido, would simply be a matter of tun-ing into the alto basso of his melodious brain and listening as it thrummed out the messages of its memory as sweetly as if it were being played on his favorite country and western radio station? He had been stupid enough to think this could be won without a battle.

As for bowing? Men of Terry Dobson's body type and patri-cian upbringing generally preferred putting a bullet in their heads to bowing. Humility was not in his genes. His aikido could be rough. He stood on your feet while insisting you roll. He ripped shirts, twisted arms, rolled farts, tickled nuts and sometimes left wrists with bracelets of pain. Prep school bullies who trained with the NY Giants for the fun of it are not known for their delicacy. But despite his early status as a bully, real violence disgusted him.

When I was in prep school I almost killed a guy on the football field. Afterwards, in the locker room, everybody congratulated me and shook my hand. I was supposed to feel proud because I had helped my team win. But I felt shamed. I knew that I had hurt this kid, and it seemed like a lousy way to live. I couldn't think of any other way. So right there I began thinking about what it is to have power, how it should be used. Now I'm no longer a little fat kid, I'm a big fat guy. It seems particularly important that men like me learn how to bow, and not just from the waist, but from the heart.

Even as a kid, he'd seen through his nature to the other side. He knew there were killing cuts that were different from cuts that could save your life. You don't cut the man, you cut the greed out of his karma. As Auden said: "I don't know why, but martial men are given to love."

My brothers and I went into the lake, and this farm kid Louie went with us. He couldn't swim. I was in the water and yelling, "Push him in, push him in. I'll save him."

So, they pushed him in. Louie panicked. When I went to grab him, he climbed up my body until he stood on my shoulders, and as he climbed, I was pushed deeper into the pond mud. Finally, he had one foot on my shoulder and another on my head. I started sinking. You know how mud sucks you under; it grips you all over.

I was under water and suddenly it occurred to me that, if Louie was standing on me, maybe there was another guy under me and I was standing on him. I could hear Louie yelling, and I could feel him thrashing around. If I looked up, I could see the light. I felt totally peaceful. I felt I could stay there forever. Louie eventually floated off me, and I yanked my legs out of the muck and got out of there. You know, the old lotus-with-its-feet-in-the-mud trip.

So, he bowed. With great struggle, he finally got his head down on his knees, his face as far into the dirt as he could manage. His offer was nonspecific, whoever was left out there to listen would do. This bow of his was going to extract an enormous price. But hadn't he already paid with thirty years of articulate and heartfelt struggle? Of doing the best he could? What was the going price for one last effort? He held his breath. He had to bow as if it were his final bow.

The world of aikido is black and white. Life and death. You should be aware of life and aware of death the moment you get on the mat. Imagine that you are on a sailing boat that had been shipwrecked. You are on a desert island, resigned to the fact that there is nothing to eat and you are going to die. A beautiful white, gleaming yacht hoves to, and a boat is sent to you. People are very nice. You had always wanted to be a sailor. The boat has sails and masts, and you can climb up and do all of these things. Your life is saved to the appearance of this vessel. All around you are nothing but sea and this yacht. There are nooks and crannies. It would take you a year to really know that vessel, much less, the people on it. Your eyes are bright from morning to night with discovery.

That's the way I was. I had a case of beginner's mind. It was unforced. If I could spend a month with that kind of head now, if I could get a beginner's mind again and see aikido as I first saw it....

While there was still enough light, there was time for one last fling at it. This time, because he knew it was going to be his last chance in this lifetime, Terry prepared himself. He stopped all his medication. He started smoking again. He announced to his students that he would be teaching his last class and they'd better show up. He put on the new Levis that he had bought at the Burlington Big 'N Tall. "I'm wanting tall," he had requested of the incredulous sales person. "I'll not be needing big." He sucked his breath in for emphasis and flicked his bright red suspenders. The suspenders hung behind him, his belly freed to wander over the waistband.

Under the portrait of Daniel Boone, the old Ashley stove was bubbling with bright heat.

I knew a guy who was a senior student of many martial arts. He took me out to the country to train. It was in the middle of winter. There was no room for us to stay in the house, so we had to sleep in the fields. It was very cold. In fact, it had snowed that night. It was much too cold to sleep. We were very tired and would occasionally nod off, but

179

the cold would soon wake us up. The inspiring moment of that night was my friend telling jokes. The stupidest, most childish jokes you could possibly imagine. We were lying in this field, three shivering bodies, screaming with laughter, covered with snow, and it just seemed very right that it should be that way. That was the way one should study, with the snow and the laughter. The two had to go together. Somehow the laughter, the snow, the darkness, and the discomfort all mingled together to be very inspiring, very right.

The next day we were stiff and sore. I wished I were any place but there. My friend said things like, "Hey, we've got a whole day to train yet!" He knew exactly how I felt, and so he would twist the knife a little bit. He would say, "Should we go get some breakfast? Or should we be real warriors and not eat anything." I'd reply, "Breakfast! Breakfast! I want some chocolate, I want some coffee, I want some ham!"

Finally, and just on time, Terry leaned into the wind. With a backward ripple of his hands, as if he were a conductor flipping the tails of his tuxedo, he turned to take on the big red IBM Selectric sitting in front of him empty as a yawn. Title for an autobiography: *Yawning in Slumber.*

And then, as if it had been lying in wait for this moment, it was suddenly dark, and he was gone. It happened over time. His voice lost timber, his laughter lost pitch, and finally, he was thin. The former 240 pounds of his body, with all its heart and muscle aches, bones, tissue, memory, its scars and its failures, fit loosely in a small ceramic urn. When it happened, the explosion was muffled and quick, unexpectedly subtle. His *ki* banged about a while before dissolving through the escape hatch in his head, taking one last gulp of the delicious air of earth before disappearing around a corner and into the roaring chest of the universe.

The Invitation

Richard Heckler

O n a hot day in early June of 1985 I was interrupted at my desk by a phone call. I was completing the final draft of a book on aikido, so I welcomed a relief from the tedium of editing.

"Hello, Richard; this is Jack Cirie. How would you like to teach aikido to the Green Berets?"

Bewildered by what I suspected was a not-so-funny joke I made a stab at a comeback.

"Yeah, sure. And how would you like to teach bowling to the Hell's Angels?"

Jack laughed: "I'm serious. We start in six weeks. Twenty-five Green Berets. You'll train them every day for six months." I was stunned. This was a challenge I had both longed for and feared. He continued: "We'll also do all of their activities with them—running, hiking, swimming, meditating, even some of their military exercises."

I suddenly felt I was being served up a meal I had ordered a long time ago. But first some background: In the early 1980s,

SportsMind—a Seattle-based organization with a successful track record among business executives as well as with athletes (Olympic, college, and professional)—was approached by the Army's Special Operations division to design an experimental program for Green Beret A-Teams. As unlikely as it seems, the Army pictured a holistic approach for enhancing the skills of individual soldiers. After three years of developing such a radical concept, designing a six-month plan of instruction, and then guiding it through the labeled bureaucratic maze, SportsMind had its brainstorm approved and funded by the Department of Defense. A senior officer who had supported the venture baptized it with the code name *The Trojan Warrior Project.* He was onto something—that soldiers initiated in this way, perhaps like the Greek warriors hidden in the belly of a wooden horse, would be an elite cadre converted to the leading edge of inner technologies, in the belly of the U.S. Army. They took the logo of a flying horse above two crossed light sabers; underneath was the inscription, *Vi Cit Tecum,* Latin for "May The Force Be With You."

Based on my experience as an aikidoist and psychologist, I was being asked to become part of the three-man core team within this program. I would also be partly responsible for organizing a one-month meditation retreat and a section called "psychological values." My two colleagues would be entrusted with a variety of tasks, including the administration of the program, biofeedback and mental training, physical fitness, diet, and also some of the so-called psychological values.

The offer was basic and unambiguous because the required involvement would be nothing less than total. Our life would become the life of the Special Forces soldiers, attending every activity, including their military exercises, with sixteen-hour days the rule.

When Jack gave me the chance to become part of this project, I immediately felt a resounding "Yes!" emerge from the core of my belly. There was no way I could turn down such an invitation. My life would be interrupted, and I would have to rearrange the next eight months with my children and former wife (as well as explain to clients why I would be gone, choose teachers to take my aikido classes, and find someone to live in my house and take care of my animals); yet I felt grateful for the opportunity. This would be the first school in the Army with a curriculum based on the holistic model—optimal performance of all human aspects: mind, body, and spirit. I would be able to teach an advanced martial art to a group of highly trained soldiers, thus, get to study firsthand a subject that had fascinated me for as long as I could remember: warriorhood and the modern warrior. It *was* the meal that I had ordered. After I accepted, I was overwhelmed by what I had to do to get ready, though sustained initially by a mild state of euphoria. It took only a day for me to be jolted into the other reality.

"How do you feel about teaching meditation to trained killers?" Andrea's pale blue eyes were filled with contempt and accusation. Her tone read like a plague warning: This man is ill for what he's about to do.

"Wait a minute," I responded, "this is an opportunity and challenge to teach the aikido version of warriorship to the military."

"It's a male ego trip," she snapped back. "What are you trying to prove to yourself anyway? To think that you would even *consider* teaching aikido to the military shocks me."

I was taken aback, but it was a paradox I would eventually have to confront, both in myself and from others. Andrea is an old and dear friend who is a Berlin psychotherapist. She accused me of being immoral for taking part in this training, and after an evening of heated discussion I found myself countering that she was one of the most hostile people that I knew, hiding behind a passive/aggressive facade of spirituality.

Staying up most of that night we launched a dialogue that continued for me with friends and colleagues over weeks. Their images of what I was doing emerged like *National Enquirer* head-lines: "Rambo Learns Mind Control!"; "I Meditated With Twenty-five Green Berets and Lived To Tell About It?"; "Special Forces Killers Trained In Human Potential Techniques!" Those that were most openly critical assumed that it would be a disaster to trans-mit awareness techniques to the Army. They argued that the mil-itary would use them for destruction, that I would merely refine their methods of aggression and make them more sinister. They reminded me that my students, after all, would be the Army's elite, "Be All That You Can Be" to the tenth power, already trained to be the instrument of force for our political process. In the eyes of some of my friends I had become a demon of their most hor-rible nightmare, Public Enemy Number One: "How could you pass these sacred teachings to *Them?*"

Us and Them. Here was a caste system of which I hadn't been consciously aware. In my mind the soldiers were not *Them.* Teach-ing the disciplines that have most positively affected me, to a population that seemed most obviously in need of them, was an obvious outgrowth of my work, obvious to me if not to others. Although I knew I would get a reaction from being part of this project, I thought it would be entirely different from the Us/ Them scenario.

The issue I first struggled with revolved around the interven-tionist policies of our government and its hostile use of the mil-itary in places I thought it shouldn't be. Coming of age during the Vietnam War, I felt forever cautioned against our country's intrusion in foreign wars. By teaching the Special Forces, would I be in effect supporting an imperialistic policy that we are now extending to Central America? Would I simply be a piece of fuel on the fires of our nation's aggressive and paranoid posturing? Would involving myself in this program make me a representa-tive of the part of our government that I most oppose? Or would I be able to express my ideals of warriorship within the military context? Could the principles of aikido add a needed dimension to our limited concept of national defense?

Almost everyone who was opposed to my teaching in this program voiced very different considerations from my own. It wasn't our foreign policy; it was Us and Them. They are bad people. If we associate with Them, we'll be tainted. We're better human beings than Them. We're different from Them, therefore they cannot be trusted. I could see that in some way my friends felt hurt or betrayed by my choice. Meditation and therapy had taught us the timeless message that compassion is right and harming others is wrong; aikido, as opposed to the martial arts that stress competition and fighting, emphasizes the loving protection of life. How, asked my friends, could I teach this power form to Them, men who might use it for harmful means?

I was shocked. What did they mean *Them?* Are these men different in kind from myself? Won't they be the same men that I played basketball with, marched with in the Marines, knew in martial arts dojos, double-dated with? Was it only because I was raised in a military family and had worn the uniform myself that I think this? Was it because I have known many men in many different situations, some good, some bad, some I liked, some I would never want to see again, that I understood that these men would be different in degree, but never in kind?

Wasn't it important that these men—*especially these men*—be exposed to the contemplative and martial arts that teach the power of harmony and wakefulness? They were the buddies, the guys I had known from childhood growing up in San Diego. I wanted to encounter them again and bring them what I had learned. I even wanted to find out why they were in the Special Forces and what they thought about warriorship.

I wasn't afraid of them. I was more afraid of those who continue to make the same terrible choices in our foreign and military policy. The men in the military, after all, are the chess pieces who carry out policy. They aren't subhuman, or even different from me. I had long wanted to begin a discussion of these issues with them. This was my opportunity.

For instance, if I were asked to teach aikido to those in the White House I would do it without question. Likewise, if I were asked to teach aikido to the Soviet Politburo. . . . I would teach it to senior citizens. I would—and have—taught it to urban gangs, chronic juvenile offenders, police officers, corporate executives, and emotionally disturbed children. Did that make me an "aikido mercenary"? Was I hero or fool?

Both sides of this issue were certainly real, and even as I tried to bolster my position by arguing that Master Morihei Ueshiba, the founder of aikido, taught the Japanese military and police, I felt a residual hollowness in my argument. More and more I began to see that I had fewer answers and more questions. I only knew that I had been given a choice to act.

When I would voice these hopes and aspirations, I would often be met by either outright opposition and slander, or a stony silence. I was told I was too idealistic, naive, or downright traitorous. I was accused of crossing over a line many of my friends felt I shouldn't have even been close to. On the eve of my departure the students at my aikido school honored me with a farewell party and presented me with a traveling bag as a gift. George Leonard, my long-time colleague and friend, gave a speech declaring that I "was taking the work from the Tamalpais Aikido dojo into the dragon's mouth." He voiced his clear support for introducing the values of aikido into the code of warriors known as the Green Berets.

Then the people I was closest to, those who had shared my highest and most difficult moments in aikido and life, shook my hand, slapped me on the back, and wished me well. It was a warm and supportive occasion, but inside I felt empty and alone. I thought of Joseph Conrad's hero in the *Heart of Darkness* who was inexorably drawn "to face the abomination."

There is certainly a legacy that distinguishes the warrior from war. The sacred path of the warrior is part of an ancient moral tradition. It includes the Indian warriors Krishna and Arjuna in the *Bhagavad-Gita;* Homer's hero Odysseus who outwitted his opponents rather than slaying them; the post-sixteenth-century Japanese Samurai who, in his finest hour, administered a peaceful government while still maintaining a personal discipline and integrity through not only the martial arts but the fine arts of calligraphy, flower arranging, and poetry. It includes the American Indians who lived in harmony with the land and whose ritual wars were exercises in bravery rather than slaughter; the Shambhala Warrior of ancient Tibet who applied power virtues to spiritual development; and Carlos Castaneda's celebrated warrior shaman, Don Juan Matus. These historical and mythical warriors found their strength and integrity by defeating their own inner demons, living in harmony with nature, and serving their fellow man. I believed—and still believe—that if we embody the virtues of these archetypal warriors, we are acting in support of the whole planet instead of constantly fighting external enemies for petty ends.

The tasks of packing, renting my house, completing my current work with clients from my psychotherapy practice, and finishing my aikido book were all relatively easy compared to saying goodbye to my children. I explained to Django, who now calls himself D.J., and Tiphani what I was going to do, and I invited them to come with me. At fourteen Tiphani didn't want to leave her friends, and D.J., age six, preferred to stay with his sister and mother. I felt remorseful about leaving them and imagined myself walking in my own father's footsteps. It was a tearful farewell, and with a lump in my throat I promised to write and call. Looking out of the airplane window at the parched brown hills of the San Francisco Bay Area, I wondered who I would be when I returned.

Contributors

Bira Almeida is the author of *Capoeira: A Brazilian Art Form*. He is a 1994 nominee for the Tinker Visiting Professorship at the University of Wisconsin at Madison by the Committee for the Study of African Diaspora. He is also the founder of Capoeira Arts Cafe in Berkeley, California, a Brazilian cultural center and capoeira academy.

Rene Denfeld is a freelance journalist and is the author of *The New Victorians* and *Kill the Body, The Head Will Fall*. She trains as an amateur boxer.

Ben Downing has published poems, essays, and reviews in *The Yale Review, Poetry Ireland, Poetry, The New Criterion, The Nation, The Paris Review, Southwest Review,* and elsewhere. He is the managing editor of *Parnassus: Poetry in Review.*

Jeff Finder has been practicing martial arts for over twenty-five years. He holds black belts in kenpo and Chinese chuan fa and is a guro in serrada escrima which he has taught in the San Francisco Bay area since 1986. He received his training as private student of the late grandmaster Angel Cabales.

John F. Gilbey is the pseudonym for Robert W. Smith, who has authored fourteen books on martial arts in the last thirty years. During his service as an officer of the Central Intelligence Agency, Smith's overseas assignments afforded him the opportunities to study the martial disciplines of the world. He has reviewed books for a wide variety of newspapers, including *The Washington Post* and the *Cleveland Plain Dealer*. His forthcoming book is *Martial Musings*.

Richard Grossinger received a B.A. from Amherst College in 1966 and a Ph.D. in Anthropology from the University of Michigan in 1975. He is the author of many books, including *Planet Medicine: Origins, Planet Medicine: Modalities, The Night Sky, Getting Made: Species, Gender and Identity* and *New Moon*. His most recent book is *Out of Babylon*.

Richard Strozzi Heckler has a fifth-degree black belt in aikido and holds ranks in judo, jiujutsu and capoeira. He has two aikido schools in the San Francisco area, and is the co-founder of The Lomi School and the Rancho Strozzi Institute, education and consulting companies that apply somatic and martial art principles to business and leadership development. He has consulted for the Army Special Forces, the U.S. Marines, the Navy SEALS, AT&T, Microsoft, Olympic athletes and urban gang members.

Riki Moss is a visual artist and writer currently working on a fictionalized biography of the late aikidoist Terry Dobson, *The Obese White Gentleman in No Uncommon Distress*. She lives in Somerville, Massachusetts.

Leonard J. Pellman has more than thirty years training and teaching experience in martial arts, including nearly ten years in Muso Jikiden Eishin-Ryu Iaijutsu. He currently serves on the Board of Directors of the Nippon Kobudo Jikishin-Kai USA, and heads the member Seishin-Kan Dojo in San Diego, California.

George Plimpton is the editor of the international literary quarterly, *The Paris Review*. He has written many books, many in the category of sports-*Paper Lion, Out of My League, Shadow Box,* and *Open Net* among them. His most recent book is *Truman Capote*.

Masayuki Shimabukuro is a seventh dan in Muso Jikiden Eishin-Ryu Iaijutsu and holds a Kyoshi title from the Dai Nippon Butoku-Kai. With nearly forty years of martial arts training and instructing experience, he is chairman of the Nippon Kobudo Jikishin-Kai USA, as well as the international branch, both of which strive to raise knowledge about Eishin-Ryu worldwide.

Ron Sieh founded the Minneapolis School of Internal Martial Arts and currently teaches t'ai chi ch'uan and general internal martial practice in the San Francisco Bay area. He is the author of *T'ai Chi Ch'uan: The Internal Tradition,* as well as *Martial Arts For Beginners.*

Bruce Thomas is best-known as the bass player for Elvis Costello and the Attractions. He is also a prolific session musician, having recorded with artists like Paul McCartney and Suzanne Vega. His critically acclaimed first novel, *The Big Wheel,* was short-listed for the Ralph J. Gleason prize for music writing. He has trained with the late kung fu master, Derek Jones, in London.

Carol A. Wiley studied martial arts for sixteen years and holds second-degree black belts in tae kwon do and aikido. She is the editor of two North Atlantic anthologies, *Women in the Martial Arts* and *Martial Arts Teachers on Teaching.* Carol also avidly pursues contact improvisation dance and is a licensed massage therapist in Bellevue, Washington.